RECENT ADVANCES ON META-HEURISTICS AND THEIR APPLICATION TO REAL SCENARIOS

Edited by **Javier Del Ser**

Recent Advances on Meta-Heuristics and Their Application to Real Scenarios

http://dx.doi.org/10.5772/3434
Edited by Javier Del Ser

Contributors

Fernando Francisco Sandoya, Dalessandro Vianna, Igor Carlos Pulini, Carlos Bazilio Martins, Alejandra Cruz-Bernal, Ikou Kaku, Patrick Siarry, Cédric Leboucher, Hyo-Sang Shin, Stéphane Le Ménec, Antonios Tsourdos, Rachid Chelouah

Published by InTech

Janeza Trdine 9, 51000 Rijeka, Croatia

Publishing Process Manager Sandra Bakic
Typesetting InTech DTP Team
Cover InTech Design Team

Additional hard copies can be obtained from orders@intechopen.com

Recent Advances on Meta-Heuristics and Their Application to Real Scenarios, Edited by Javier Del Ser
p. cm.
ISBN 978-953-51-0913-6

For EU product safety concerns:
IN TECH d.o.o., Prolaz Marije Krucifikse Kozulić 3, 51000 Rijeka, Croatia,
info@intechopen.com or visit our website at intechopen.com.

Meet the editor

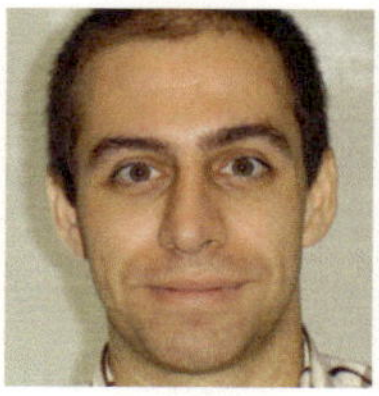

Javier (Javi) Del Ser is the technology manager of the OPTIMA (Optimization, Modelling and Analytics) business area at TECNALIA RESEARCH & INNOVATION (www.tecnalia.com). He achieved his Ph.D. degree (cum laude) in Electrical Engineering from the University of Navarra (Spain) in 2006, and will get his second PhD in Information Technology from the University of Alcalá (Spain) in early 2013. He has held different positions in the University of Navarra and University of Mondragon (Spain), as well as visiting stays at the University of Delaware (USA) and VTT (Finland). His research interests lie on data analytics and heuristic algorithms for wireless sensor networks, economics, operational research and resource allocation. He has published more than 120 contributions to journals and conferences, edited 2 books, invented 4 patents, and led several research projects. Dr. Del Ser is a senior member of the IEEE, and has recently been awarded the "Talent of Bizkaia" prize for his outstanding professional curriculum.

Contents

Preface

The last decade has witnessed a sharp increase in the dimensionality of different underlying optimization paradigms stemming from a variety of fields and scenarios. Examples abound not only in what relates to purely technological sectors, but also in other multiple disciplines, ranging from bioinformatics to finance, economics, operational research, logistics, social and food sciences, among many others. Indeed, almost every single aspect driving this increased dimensionality has grown exponentially as exemplified by the upsurge of communication terminals for the optimization of cellular network planning or the rising need for sequence alignment, analysis, and annotation in genomics.

As a result, the computational complexity derived from solving all such paradigms in an optimal fashion has augmented accordingly, to the extent of igniting an active research trend towards near-optimal yet cost-efficient heuristic solvers. Broadly speaking, heuristics resort to experience-based approximate techniques for solving problems when enumerative alternatives (e.g. exhaustive search) are not efficient due to the high computational complexity derived therefrom. In particular, meta-heuristics have lately gained momentum, conceived as heuristics springing from the mimicking of intelligent learning procedures and behaviours observed in Nature, arts and social sciences. As such, from the advent of genetically-inspired search algorithms in mid 70s, a wide portfolio of evolutionary meta-heuristics and techniques based on the so-called swarm intelligence has been applied to distinct optimization paradigms: to mention a few, harmony search, memetic algorithms, differential search, ant colony optimization, particle swarm optimization, cuckoo search, gravitational search, intelligent water drops, coral reef optimization and simulated annealing, among many others.

This flurry of activity around meta-heuristics and their application to real scenarios is the raison d'être of this booklet: to provide the reader with an insightful report on advances in meta-heuristic techniques in certain exemplifying scenarios. On this purpose, the booklet comprises 5 chapters, each presenting the application of different meta-heuristics to different scenarios. The first chapter addresses the application of multi-objective genetic algorithms for optimizing the task scheduling of garment companies. The approach takes three conflicting objectives into account: to minimize the total production time, to maximize the percentage of use of corporate production centers and to minimize the internal production centers downtime. Next, the second chapter proposes to hybridize the so-called greedy randomized adaptive search procedure (GRASP) with path relinking for optimally selecting work teams under maximum diversity criteria, with clear applications to operational research, academia and politics. The third chapter delves into a thorough review on meta-heuristics applied to the route finding problem in robotics, with an emphasis on the combination of genetic algorithms and ant colony optimization as an outperforming scheme with respect to other existing approaches. On the other hand, the fourth chapter investigates different meta-heuristic algorithms in the context of multilevel lot-sizing problems, which hinge on determining the lot sizes for producing/procuring multiple items at different levels with quantitative interdependencies, so as to minimize the total production costs in the planning horizon. This chapter also introduces a special variable neighborhood based algorithm shown to perform satisfactorily for several simulated benchmark instances under diverse scales. Finally, the fifth chapter ends the booklet by outlining a two-step optimization method for dynamic weapon target assignment problem, a military-driven application where an allocation plan is to be found to assigning the available weapons in an area to incoming targets. Specifically, the proposed scheme combines different optimization approaches such as graph theory, evolutionary game theory, and particle swarm optimization.

The editor would like to eagerly thank the authors for their contribution to this book, and especially the editorial assistance provided by the InTech publishing process manager, Ms. Natalia Reinic. Last but not least, the editor's gratitude extends to the anonymous manuscript processing team for their arduous formatting work.

Dr. Javier Del Ser
Technology Manager, OPTIMA Business Area
TECNALIA RESEARCH & INNOVATION
Zamudio, Spain

Chapter 1

Using Multiobjective Genetic Algorithm and Multicriteria Analysis for the Production Scheduling of a Brazilian Garment Company

Dalessandro Soares Vianna, Igor Carlos Pulini and Carlos Bazilio Martins

Additional information is available at the end of the chapter

http://dx.doi.org/10.5772/53701

1. Introduction

The Brazilian garment industry has been forced to review its production processes due to the competition against Asiatic countries like China. These countries subsidize the production in order to generate employment, which reduces the production cost. This competition has changed the way a product is made and the kind of production. The industry has focused on customized products rather than the ones large-scale produced. This transformation has been called "mass customization" [1].

In this scenario the Brazilian garment industry has been forced to recreate its production process to provide a huge diversity of good quality and cheaper products. These must be made in shorter periods and under demand. These features require the use of chronoanalysis to analyze the production load balance. Since the production time becomes crucial, the task[1] allocation must regard the distinct production centers[2]. Most of a product lead time – processing time from the beginning to the end of the process – is spent waiting for resources. In the worse case, it can reach 80% of the total time [2]. So the production load balance is critical to acquire a good performance.

It is hard to accomplish production load balance among distinct production centers. This balance must regards the available resources and respect the objectives of the production.

1 Tasks: set of operations taken on the same production phase.

2 Production centers: internal or external production cell composed by a set of individuals which are able to execute specific tasks.

Lindem [3] argues that these scheduling problems are NP-Complete since the search space is a factorial of the number of variables. These problems may be solved by using exact methods. However due to time constraints, heuristics must be used in order to find good quality solutions within a reasonable time.

Nowadays the ERP (Enterprise Resource Planning) systems used by the Brazilian garment industry do not consider the finite source of resources and the constraints of the real production environment [3]. Task scheduling is done manually through simple heuristics techniques like FIFO (First In First Out) and SPT (Shortest Processing Time). Although those techniques can generate feasible solutions, these ones usually have poor quality.

In real optimization problems, as the problem addressed in this work, is generally desirable to optimize more than one performance objective at the same time. These objectives are generally conflicting, i.e., when one objective is optimized, the others become worse. The goal of multiobjective combinatorial optimization (MOCO) [4] [5] is to optimize simultaneously more than one objective. MOCO problems have a set of optimal solutions (instead of a single optimum) in the sense that no other solutions are superior to them when all objectives are taken into account. They are known as *Pareto optimal* or *efficient* solutions.

Solving MOCO problems is quite different from single-objective case, where an optimal solution is searched. The difficulty is not only due to the combinatorial complexity as in single-objective case, but also due to the research of all elements of the efficient set, whose cardinality grows with the number of objectives.

In the literature, some authors have proposed exact methods for solving specific MOCO problems, which are generally valid to bi-objective problems but cannot be adapted easily to a higher number of objectives. Also, the exact methods are inefficient to solve large-scale NP-hard MOCO problems. As in the single-objective case, the use of heuristic/metaheuristic techniques seems to be the most promising approach to MOCO problems because of their efficiency, generality and relative simplicity of implementation [5] [6] [7]. Genetic algorithms are the most commonly used metaheuristic in the literature to solve these problems [8].

The objective of this work is to develop a method to carry out the production scheduling of a Brazilian garment company, placed at Espírito Santo state, in real time, which must regularly balance the product demands with the available resources. This is done in order to: reduce the total production time; prioritize the use of internal production centers of the company rather than the use of external production centers; and reduce the downtime of the internal production centers.

With this purpose, initially a mixed integer programming model was developed for the problem. Then, we implemented a multiobjective genetic algorithm (MGA) based on the NSGA-II [4] model, which generates a set of sub-optimal solutions to the addressed problem. After we used the multicriteria method Weighted Sum Model – WSM [9] to select one of the solutions obtained by the MGA to be applied to the production scheduling. The mixed integer programming model, the MGA developed and its automatic combination with the multicriteria method WSM are original contributions of this work.

2. Addressed problem

The production planning process of the Brazilian garment industry may be split into many phases from demand provision to tasks scheduling at each machine. Tubino [2] says that the production planning is defined by the demand from the Planning Master of Production (PMP). This demand is sent to the Material Requirements Planning (MRP) that calculates the material required. Then it becomes available to the Issuance of Production Orders and Sequencing. These steps are depicted at Figure 1.

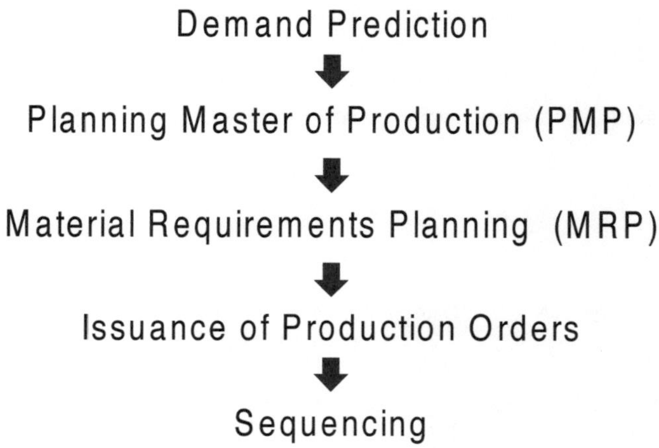

Figure 1. Production planning.

This work approaches the scheduling phase where a set of tasks has to be distributed among production centers. As said before, production center is an internal or external production cell composed by a set of specialized individuals. Each task may be done by a set of production centers and each production center is able to execute many tasks. The objectives of this work are: i) to minimize the total production time (*makespan* – time from the beginning of the first task to the end of the last task); ii) to maximize the use of internal production centers – the use of internal production centers does not imply cost overhead[3] since employees' salary are already at the payroll of the company; iii) to minimize the internal production centers downtime.

These three objectives have been chosen in order to meet the needs of the analyzed company. Some couple of them are conflicting, i.e., when one has an improvement the other tends to get worse. Others objectives are not conflicting, but the optimization of one does not guarantee the optimization of the other. As an example of conflicting objectives, we have the objectives "to minimize the total production time" and "to maximize the use of internal production centers": for minimizing the total production time it is necessary to make the best use of the available production centers, regardless of whether they are internal or exter-

3 Except when the company has to pay overtime.

nal. The objectives "to minimize the total production time" and "to minimize the internal production centers downtime" are not conflicting: by decreasing the downtime of the production centers, the total production time also tends to decrease. However, if tasks are allocated to an internal production center, which together have an execution time shorter than the total production time, it is possible to arrange them in different ways without changing the total production time. The objective "to minimize the internal production centers downtime" requires the best arrangement of the tasks within each internal production center.

In order to better describe the addressed problem, Figure 2 depicts the steps toward the production of a short. The production process is composed by a set of production stages. Each stage has a set of operations to be performed. In this work, this set is called task. In this example, there are 6 production stages (scratch, cut, sewing, embroidery, laundry and finishing). The sewing task lasts 12.54 minutes and is composed by d operations. There are h production centers qualified to perform the sewing task.

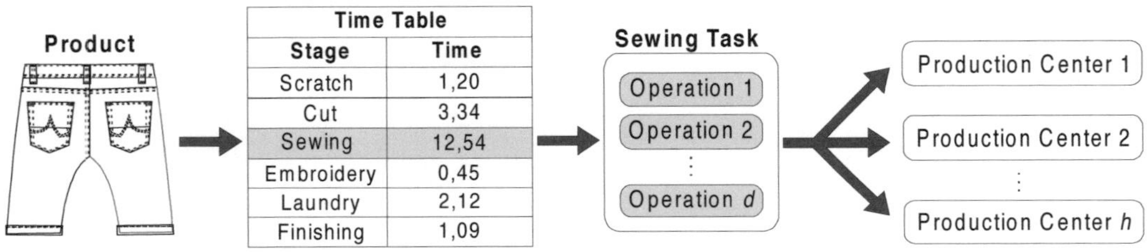

Figure 2. Example of a production process.

The execution time of a task is the sum of the execution time of its operations. This time is used during the scheduling, which hides the complexity of the operation distribution inside a stage. So it can be seen as a classical task scheduling where each production center is a machine and the operations set of each production stage is a task.

During the scheduling process the following constraints must be respected: i) for each product exists an execution order of tasks, i.e., there is a precedence order among tasks; ii) each task can only be executed in production centers that are qualified to it, i.e. production centers are specialized; iii) employees stop working regularly for lunch and eventually for others reasons like training or health care; iv) depending on the workload it is possible to work overtime; v) the time spent to go from one to another production center must be considered.

The addressed problem is similar to the flexible job shop problem, in which there is a set of work centers that groups identical machines operating concurrently; inside a work center, a task may be executed by any of the machines available [10]. Figure 3 depicts an example of adapting the flexible job shop to the addressed problem. In this figure, three products are made: Product 1 requires tasks T_{11}, T_{12}, T_{13}, T_{14}, T_{15} and T_{16}; Product 2 requires tasks T_{21}, T

$_{22}$, T_{23}, T_{25} and T_{26}; Product 3 requires tasks T_{31}, T_{32}, T_{33}, T_{34} and T_{36}. All tasks are distributed among production centers C_1, C_2, C_3, C_4 and C_5.

In Figure 3 the problem is divided into 2 subproblems: A and B. At subproblem A the tasks are distributed among the production centers that can execute them. At this step is important to prioritize internal production centers in order to take profit of the company processing power that is already available. At subproblem B the tasks must be scheduled respecting the precedence order of tasks.

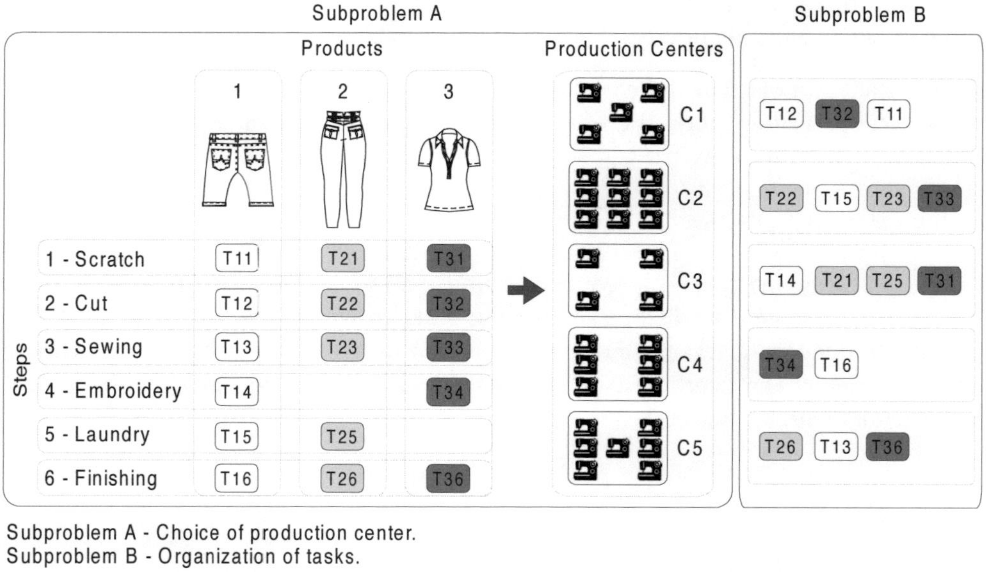

Figure 3. Task distribution among the production centers.

Figure 4(1) depicts an example of scheduling for the tasks listed in Figure 3. Note that the precedence relation among tasks is respected, that is, a task T_{ij}, where i means the product to be made and j the production stage, can be started only after all tasks T_{ik} ($k < j$) have been finished. The Figure 4(2) shows the downtime (gray arrows) in the production centers. For instance, task T_{13} at production center C_5 waits for the task T_{12} at C_3 before starts executing. Figure 4(3) shows that the tasks T_{25} and T_{31} at production center C_1 and T_{38} at C_5 (black boxes) were ready but had to be frozen because of the unavailability of the production centers C_1 and C_5.

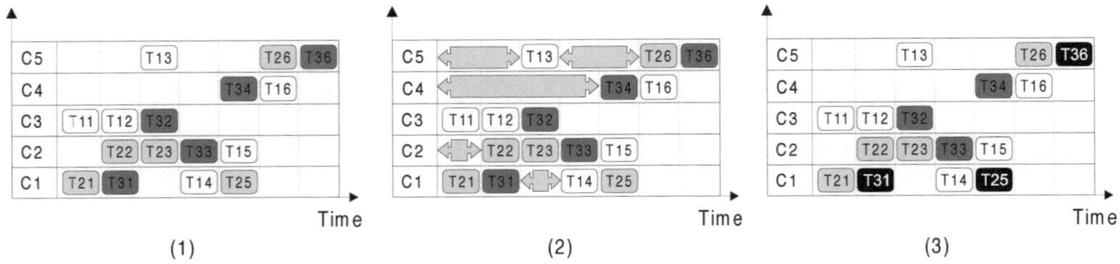

Figure 4. Example of tasks scheduling.

The addressed problem is similar to some works found in the literature, like Senthilkumar and Narayanan [11], Santosa, Budiman and Wiratino [12], Abdelmaguid [13], Dayou, Pu and Ji [14], Chang and Chyu [15] and Franco [16]. However, these works do not consider real-time tasks sequencing or are not applied to real problems.

It is important to note that the chronoanalysis method used here is not the focus of this work. However, in this work, the production time includes tolerance, rhythm and others variables from the chronoanalysis.

2.1. Mathematical modeling

For this modeling was created a sequencing unit (*SU*) which defines a time-slice of work. Each production center has distinct sequencing units, in which tasks are scheduled all day long. Figure 5 depicts a set of sequencing units that describes the behavior of a particular production center. The overtime work is treated as a distinct sequencing unit, since they have particular features like cost.

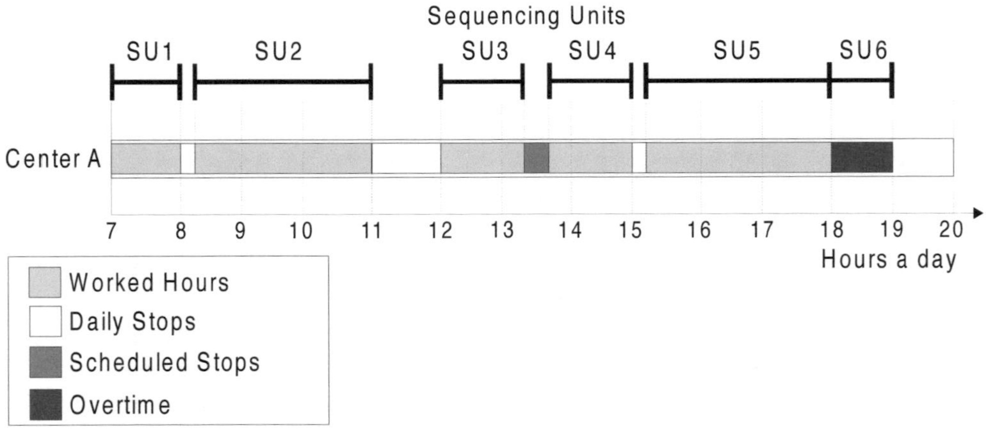

Figure 5. Sequencing units organization.

This model defines a variable N that indicates the total number of tasks, including an additional task that is required for the initialization of the sequencing units.

Below is presented the mixed integer programming model for the addressed problem. The parameters of the problem are presented, followed by the interval indexes, the decision variables and finally by the equations for the three objective functions together with their constraints.

Parameters

NCP – Number of production centers.

NSU – Number of sequencing units.

NJ – Number of tasks to be scheduled.

N – Total number of tasks ($N = NJ + 1$). The last one is the fictitious task that was added to the model as the initial task of every sequencing unit.

M – Large enough value.

WL_i – Workload of task i.

CP_s – Production center of the sequencing unit s.

$Minimum_s$ – Starting time of the sequencing unit s.

$Time_s$ – Amount of time available at sequencing unit s.

CPJ_i – Set of production centers that can execute the task i.

CI – Set of internal production centers.

PRE_i – Set of tasks that are a precondition for the execution of task i.

$OffSet_{c_k c_l}$ – Time for going from production center c_k to c_l.

Indexes

i, j – Indexes of tasks. $i, j \in [1, N]$.

c – Index of production centers. $c \in [1, NCP]$.

s – Indexes of sequencing units. $s \in [1, NSU]$.

Decision variables

$Start_i$ – Non-negative linear variable that represents the starting time of task i.

End_i – Non-negative linear variable that represents the ending time of task i.

WLS_{si} – Non-negative linear variable that represents the workload of task i at the sequencing unit s.

$StartS_{si}$ – Non-negative linear variable that represents the starting time of task i at sequencing unit s.

DT_{sij} – Non-negative linear variable that represents the downtime between tasks i and j in the sequencing unit s.

Y_{sij} – Non-negative linear variable that represents the flow i, j of the sequencing unit s.

MkSpan – Non-negative linear variable that represents the time between the end of the last finished task and the start of the first task.

IntTime – Non-negative linear variable that represents the amount of execution time of tasks in the internal production centers.

DownTime – Non-negative linear variable that represents the amount of internal production centers downtime.

$$Z_{ci} = \begin{cases} 1 & \text{if task } i \text{ is allocated to production center } c. \\ 0 & \text{otherwise} \end{cases}$$

$$U_{si} = \begin{cases} 1 & \text{if task } i \text{ is allocated to sequencing unit } s. \\ 0 & \text{otherwise} \end{cases}$$

$$X_{sij} = \begin{cases} 1 & \text{if the sequence } i,\ j \text{ happens in the sequencing unit } s. \\ 0 & \text{otherwise} \end{cases}$$

Model

$$O.F.1 = Min \quad MkSpan \tag{1}$$

$$O.F.2 = Max \quad IntTime \tag{2}$$

$$O.F.3 = Min \quad DownTime \tag{3}$$

Subject to:

$$MkSpan \geq End_i \quad \forall i / i \neq N \tag{4}$$

$$IntTime = \sum_{s/CP_s \in CI} \sum_{i/i \neq N} WLS_{si} \tag{5}$$

$$DownTime = \sum_{s/CP_s \in CI} \sum_{i} \sum_{j/j \neq N} DT_{sij} \tag{6}$$

$$DT_{sij} \geq StartS_{sj} - (StartS_{si} + WLS_{si}) - M \times (1 - X_{sij}) \tag{7}$$

$$\sum_{i/CP_s \in CPJ_i} Y_{sij} - \sum_{i/i \neq N, CP_s \in CPJ_i} Y_{sji} = U_{sj} \quad \forall s, \forall j / j \neq N \, and \quad CP_s \in CPJ_j \tag{8}$$

$$Y_{sij} \le M \times X_{sij} \quad \forall s, \forall i / CP_s \in CPJ_i, \forall j / j \ne N \, and \quad CP_s \in CPJ_j \tag{9}$$

$$U_{sN} = 1 \quad \forall s \tag{10}$$

$$\sum_{c/c \in CPJ_i} Z_{ci} = 1 \quad \forall i / i \ne N \tag{11}$$

$$\sum_{s/CP_s \in CPJ_i} U_{si} \ge 1 \quad \forall i \tag{12}$$

$$U_{si} \le Z_{ci} \quad \forall i, \forall s / CP_s \in CPJ_i, c = CP_s \tag{13}$$

$$\sum_{i/CP_s \in CPJ_i} X_{sij} = U_{sj} \quad \forall s, \forall j / j \ne N \, and \quad CP_s \in CPJ_j \tag{14}$$

$$\sum_{j/j \ne N, CP_s \in CPJ_j} X_{sij} \le U_{si} \quad \forall s, \forall i / i \ne N \tag{15}$$

$$StartS_{si} \ge Minimum_s \times U_{si} \quad \forall s / CP_s \in CPJ_i, \forall i / i \ne N \tag{16}$$

$$StartS_{si} + WLS_{si} \le Minimim_s + Time_s + M \times (1 - U_{si}) \quad \forall s, \forall i / i \ne N \quad and \quad CP_s \in CPJ_i \tag{17}$$

$$\sum_{s/CP_s = c, CP_s \in CPJ_i} WLS_{si} = WL_{ci} * Z_{ci} \quad \forall i, \forall c \tag{18}$$

$$WLS_{si} \le M \times U_{si} \quad \forall s / CP_s \in CPJ_i, \forall i \tag{19}$$

$$Start_i \le StartS_{si} + M \times (1 - U_{si}) \quad \forall s / CP_s \in CPJ_i, \forall i \tag{20}$$

$$End_i \le StartS_{si} + WLS_{si} - M \times (1 - U_{si}) \quad \forall s / CP_s \in CPJ_i, \forall i \tag{21}$$

$$End_i \ge Start_i \quad \forall i / i \ne N \tag{22}$$

$$StartS_{sj} \ge StartS_{si} + WLS_{si} - M \times (1 - X_{sij}) \quad \forall s, \forall i / CP_s \in CPS_i, \forall j / j \ne N \quad and \quad CP_s \in CPJ_j \tag{23}$$

$$Start_j \ge End_i + OffSet_{c_1 c_2} - M \times (2 - Z_{c_1 i} - Z_{c_2 j}) \quad \forall c_1, \forall c_2, \forall i / i \ne N \quad and \quad c_1 \in CPJ_i, \forall j / j \ne N, i \in PRE_j \, and \quad c_2 \in CPJ_j \tag{24}$$

Where:

1. Objective function that aims to minimize the total production time (*makespan*).
2. Objective function that aims to maximize the use of internal production centers.
3. Objective function that aims to minimize the amount of downtime at the internal production centers.
4. The makespan can be seen as the ending time of the last task.
5. The amount of execution time at the internal production centers.
6. The amount of downtime at the internal production centers.
7. The amount of downtime between tasks i and j in the sequencing unit s.
8. Constrains the flow between tasks i and j.
9. $X_{sij} = 1$ if there is a flow from task i to task j at the sequencing unit s.
10. Asserts that task N belongs to every sequencing unit.
11. Asserts that each task is executed on just one production center.
12. Asserts that each task is executed on at least one sequencing unit.
13. Asserts that a task i can only be executed on a sequencing unit s if the task i is scheduled to the production center of the sequencing unit s.
14. If the task j is performed in sequencing unit s then there is just one task that immediately precedes j in s.
15. If the task j is performed in sequencing unit s then there is at most one task that is immediately preceded by j in s.
16. Asserts that each task i must be started only after the start of the sequencing unit s where task i is allocated.
17. Asserts that the maximum available time of the sequencing unit is being respected.
18. Asserts that the required workload of task i is allocated.
19. Asserts that the workload of task i at the sequencing unit s is 0 (zero) if task i is not scheduled to the sequencing unit s.
20. Asserts that the beginning time of task i, $Start_i$, must be lower or equal to the beginning time of task i at any sequencing unit where it is allocated.
21. Asserts that the ending time of task i, End_i, must be greater or equal to the ending time of task i at any sequencing unit where it is allocated.
22. Asserts that the ending time of task i must be at least equal to its beginning.
23. Asserts that the task i starts only after the ending time of the task j that immediately precedes i in the sequencing unit s.

http://dx.doi.org/10.5772/53701

24. Asserts that task j only can starts after the ending time of its predecessor tasks. This restriction takes into account the travel time between the production centers.

3. Proposed method

We propose in this work a method that combines multiobjective genetic algorithm and multicriteria decision analysis for solving the addressed problem. The multiobjective genetic algorithm (MGA) aims to find a good approximation of the efficient solution set, considering the three objectives of the problem. A multicriteria decision analysis method is applied on the solution set obtained by the MGA in order to choose one solution, which will be used by the analyzed garment company.

Deb [4] presents a list of evolutionary algorithms for solving problems with multiple objectives: *Vector Evaluated GA* (VEGA); *Lexicographic Ordering GA*; *Vector Optimized Evolution Strategy* (VOES); *Weight-Based GA* (WBGA); *Multiple Objective GA* (MOGA); *Niched Pareto GA* (NPGA, NPGA 2); *Non dominated Sorting GA* (NSGA, NSGA-II); *Distance-based Pareto GA* (DPGA); *Thermodynamical GA* (TDGA); *Strength Pareto Evolutionary Algorithm* (SPEA, SPEA 2); *Mult-Objective Messy GA* (MOMGA-I, II, III); *Pareto Archived ES* (PAES); *Pareto Envelope-based Selection Algorithm* (PESA, PESA II); *Micro GA-MOEA* (μGA, μGA2); and *Multi-Objective Bayesian Optimization Algorithm* (mBOA).

In this work, we have chosen the NSGA-II [17] evolutionary algorithm since it works with any number of objectives, which can be easily added or removed. This feature facilitates the company to adapt to the market demands – the current objectives may not be sufficient in the future, requiring the company to also focus on other goals –. Besides, there are another Brazilian garment companies interested in using the proposed method, which may have different objectives.

The main methods of multicriteria decision analysis are [18]: Weighted Sum Model, Condorcet method, analytic hierarchic process, ELECTRE methods, Promethee method and MacBeth method.

The Weighted Sum Model – WSM is used in this work due to its simplicity and, mainly, due to its structure of candidates and voters. In this work, WSM performs as a decision maker by considering each solution returned by the MGA as a candidate and each objective of the problem as a voter.

The method proposed in this work is detailed in Section 3.2. But first, in Section 3.1, we describe the multiobjective combinatorial optimization, in order to facilitate the understanding of the proposed method.

3.1. Multiobjective combinatorial optimization

According to Arroyo [19], a Multiobjective Combinatorial Optimization (MOCO) problem consists of minimizing (or maximizing) a set of objectives while satisfying a set of constraints. In a MOCO problem, there is no single solution that optimizes each objective, but a set of efficient solutions in such way that no solution can be considered better than another solution for all objectives.

Among the different ways of defining an optimal solution for MOCO problems, Pitombeira [20] highlights the method proposed by the economist Vilfredo Pareto in the nineteenth century, which introduces the dominance concept. He argues that an optimal solution for a MOCO problem must have a balance between the different objective functions, so that the attempt of improving the value of one function implies the worsening of one or more of the others. This concept is called *Pareto optimal.*

MOCO aims to find the Pareto optimal set (also known as *Pareto frontier*) or the best approximation of it. However, it is necessary to define a binary relationship called *Pareto dominance*: a solution x_1 dominates another solution x_2 if the functional values of x_1 are better than or equal to the functional values of x_2 and at least one of the functional values of x_1 is strictly better than the functional value of x_2 [4]. The Pareto optimal set consists of all non-dominated solutions of the search space.

Deb [4] says that in addition to finding a solution set near to the Pareto frontier, it is necessary that these solutions are well distributed, which allows a broader coverage of the search space. This fact facilitates the decision making, because, regardless of the weight assigned to each criterion, a quality solution will be chosen.

3.2. Multiobjective genetic algorithm proposed

As we have already mentioned, the model adopted for the development of the multiobjective genetic algorithm (MGA) proposed is the NSGA-II. According to Deb [4], it is an elitist search procedure, which preserves the dominant solutions through the generations. The process starts by building a population (*P*), with *nPop* individuals (solutions). The populations of the next generations are obtained through the application of mutation, selection and crossover operators. The purpose is to find a diversified solution set near to the Pareto frontier. With the *crowding distance* [4], we can qualify the space around the solution, allowing a greater diversity of the solution set and, thereby, leading more quickly to a highest quality solution. The crowding distance (*d*) of an individual in the ith position of the population *P*, considering *r* objectives, is given by Equation 25, where f_k^{min} and f_k^{max} represent, respectively, the minimum and maximum values in *P* for the objective function f_k $(1 \leq k \leq r)$. For any solution set, the solution that brings the highest level of diversity is the one with the greatest crowding distance.

$$d_i = \frac{f_1^{(i+1)} - f_1^{(i-1)}}{f_1^{\max} - f_1^{\min}} + \frac{f_2^{(i+1)} - f_2^{(i-1)}}{f_2^{\max} - f_2^{\min}} + \dots + \frac{f_r^{(i+1)} - f_r^{(i-1)}}{f_r^{\max} - f_r^{\min}} \tag{25}$$

Section 3.2.1 presents the solution representation used in this work. The steps done by the MGA proposed, from the building of the initial population to the choice of the solution to be used by the analyzed garment company, is detailed in Section 3.2.2.

3.2.1. *Solution representation*

The solution (individual) is represented by two integer arrays: priorities array and production centers array. Tasks are represented by the indexes of both arrays. The priorities array defines the allocation sequence of the tasks and the production centers array indicates the production center responsible for the execution of each task. Figure 6 depicts an example of the solution representation used in this work, in which the first task to be allocated is the task 3 – represented by the position (index) with value 1 in the priorities array – and the production center responsible by its execution is the production center 3 – value of the position 3 of the production centers array –; the second task to be allocated is the task 7, which will be executed in the production center 5; and so on. This representation is based on the representations described in [14] [21] [22] and [23].

Index of tasks	1	2	3	4	5	6	7	8	9	10
Priorities array	7	4	1	8	10	3	2	5	9	6
Production centers array	1	1	3	2	1	2	5	2	6	5

Figure 6. Solution representation.

A task T_i can only start after the end of the predecessor task T_j plus the travel time from the production center responsible by T_i to the production center responsible by T_j. Thus, when a task is selected to be allocated, a recursive search is done in order to allocate the predecessor tasks of it.

3.2.2. *Population evolution*

The MGA proposed is described by the flowchart of Figure 7, which starts by building the initial population and finalizes when the stop criterion is reached. Mutation, selection and crossover genetic operators are applied in the current population in order to build new individuals (*offsprings*). At the end of each generation, the less evolved individuals are eliminated and the evolutionary process continues with the best individuals.

Step 1 – Building the initial population

Two arrays of size *N* are created for each individual, where *N* is the number of tasks to be allocated. The priorities array stores the allocation sequence and the production centers array determines the production center responsible for each task. These arrays are randomly created.

Step 2 – Generating the offspring population

An offspring population, P_{aux}, with *nPop* individuals is created from *P*, using the tournament selection method [24] and mutation and crossover genetic operators. The tournament method used in this work randomly selects four individuals from *P* and the best two are selected as the parent individuals to be used by the crossover operator.

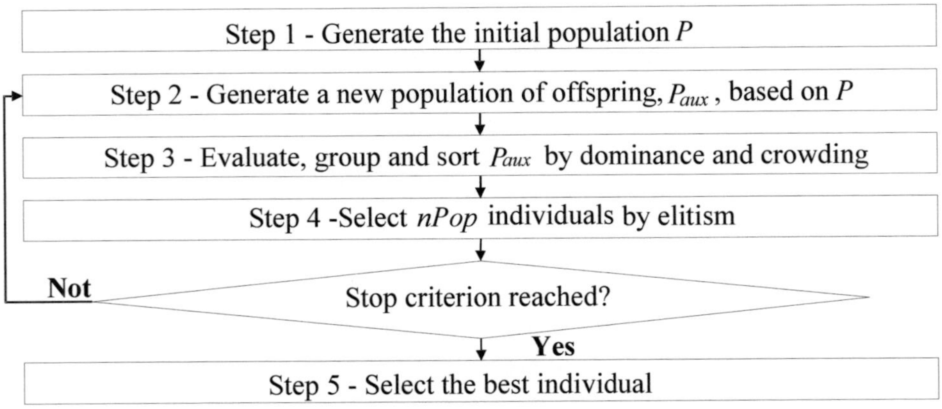

Figure 7. NSGA-II algorithm.

The crossover operator used in this work is based on the variable one-point cut operator [24]. Figure 8 depicts examples of the crossover (8a and 8b) and mutation (8c and 8d) operators developed in this work. As can been seen in Figure 8(a), the priorities array of the offspring individual is composed by the genes of the priorities array of the parent individual $Parent_1$ until the cut-point and, from this point, it is composed by the remaining priorities in the order that they appear in the priorities array of the parent individual $Parent_2$. In the production centers array, the crossover method is applied by using the same cut-point and the production centers array of the offspring individual is composed by the genes of the production centers array of the parent individual $Parent_1$ until the cut-point and, from this point, it is composed by the genes of the production centers array of the parent individual $Parent_2$, as can be visualized in Figure 8(b).

The mutation operator is applied at the priorities array as shown in Figure 8(c), where two genes are randomly selected and their contents are exchanged. The mutation operator acts in the production center array as shown in Figure 8(d), where a gene (position *i*) is randomly selected and replaced by another production center capable of execute the task *i*. This production center is randomly chosen. The mutation operator is performed on 5% of the genes of each offspring individual generated by the crossover operator.

Step 3 – Evaluation, sorting and grouping of individuals by dominance and crowding distance

The offspring population P_{aux} is added to the population P, defining a new population of $2 \times nPop$ individuals – $nPop$ individuals from P and $nPop$ individuals from P_{aux} –. It is sorted in ascending order by the dominance level[4]. The crowding distance is used as a tie-breaker, i.e., when two individuals have the same dominance level, it is chosen the one with the greatest crowding distance.

4 The dominance level of an individual x is the number of individuals in the population that dominates x; for example, an individual dominated by only one individual in the population has dominance level of 1.

Step 4 – Selection of individuals by elitism

The *nPop* best individuals from the new population (P_{aux} added to P) are selected to continue the evolutionary process, while the others are discarded.

Step 5 – Selection of the best individual

At the end of the evolutionary process, the MGA returns a set of individuals with dominance level of 0 (zero), that is, individuals of the current population that no other individual dominates. This set of individuals represents an approximation of the Pareto frontier.

The Weight Sum Model (WSM) [25] multicriteria decision method is applied for choosing a solution from the set returned by the MGA that will be used by the analyzed garment company. In the WSM method, the candidates are ranked by the preferences of the decision maker, in which the best candidate for a particular preference receives 1 (one) point, the second one receives 2 (two) points, and so on. The points received for each preference are summed, and the best candidate is the one with the smallest sum.

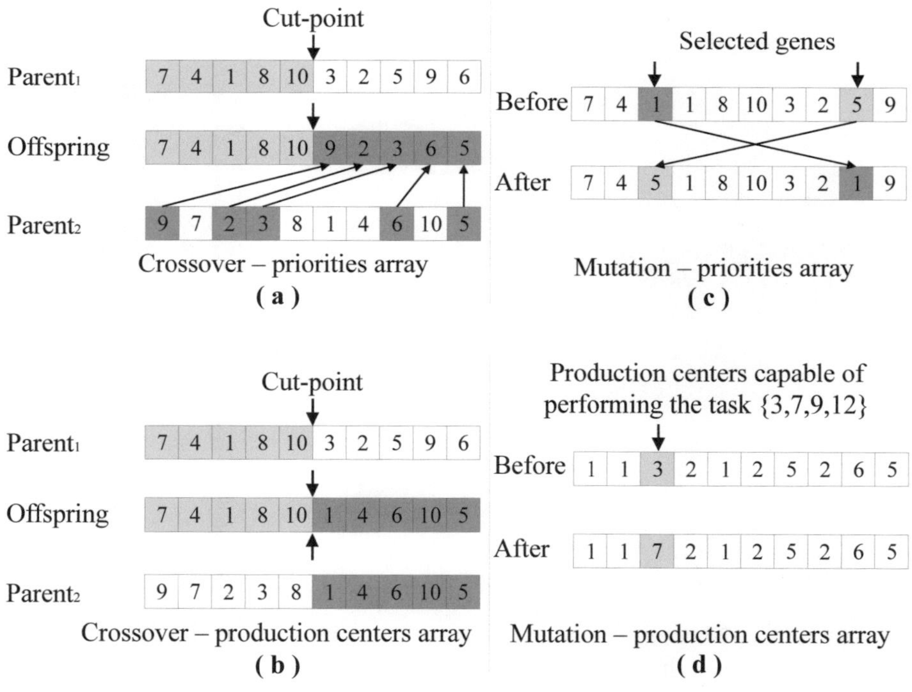

Figure 8. Genetic operators of crossover and mutation.

In this work, the WSM method replaces the grade given by the voters to the candidates. This replacement ranks each solution returned by the MGA according to each objective. Figure 9 illustrates the use of the WSM method in this work where four solutions (columns) must be evaluated according to three objectives (rows). For the first objective, to minimize the total production time (*makespan*), the solution 3 has the best value, obtaining the rank 1; the solution 4 has the best second value, obtaining the rank 2; and the solutions 1 and 2 obtain, respectively, the ranks 3 and 4. The same ranking is done for the others objectives. After summing the rank obtained for each objective, the solution 1 is chosen because it has the smallest sum.

4. Computational results

All computational experiments were performed on a Dell Vostro 3700 notebook with 1.73 GHz Intel Core I7 processor and 6 Gbytes of RAM memory.

The computation experiments regard to real data that represent the May 2012 production demand of the analyzed company: 567 products, 1511 production orders, 3937 tasks and 181 production centers.

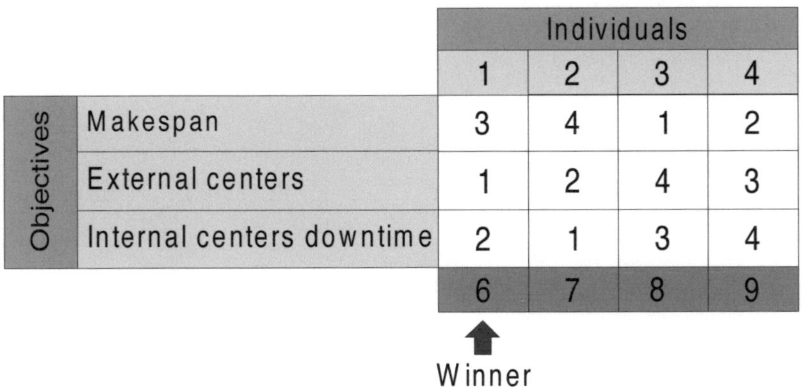

Figure 9. Weighted sum model.

In the experiments, 12 hours of execution time was established as the stop criterion of the genetic algorithm. This value was defined because it represents the available time between two work days. The population size (*nPop*) and the mutation rate (*tx*) were empirically set at *nPop*=200 individuals and *tx*=5%.

In the first experiment, we compare the results of the proposed method with the results manually obtained by the analyzed company at May 2011. Figure 10 depicts the production deviation of each stage between May 2011 and May 2012, where we can note an increase of the production at almost all stages.

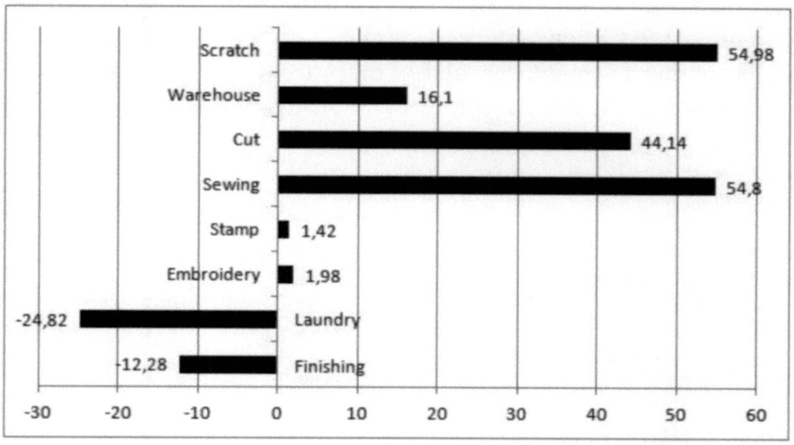

Figure 10. Production deviation of each stage (May 2011 x May 2012).

The results obtained by the analyzed company at May 2011 were: 42 production days to execute all tasks; 20% of the tasks were performed in internal production centers; and the downtime rate of the internal production centers was 37%.

In this experiment, five runs of the proposed method were done, obtaining the following average results: 36 production days to execute all tasks; 32% of the tasks were performed in internal production centers; and the downtime rate of the internal production centers was 16%. It is worth to mention that the worst results obtained are: 38 production days to execute all tasks; 35% of the tasks were performed in internal production centers; and the downtime rate of the internal production centers was 18%. The obtained results were better than the ones manually got at May 2011, even considering the increase of the production between May 2011 and May 2012 (see Figure 10).

We mean "selected solution" as the solution (individual) of the population of generation g that would be returned by the proposed method if the genetic algorithm ended at generation g. Figures 11, 12 and 13 depict the obtained values for each objective of the selected solutions during 12 hours of execution. In these figures are also used the average results obtained after five runs of the proposed method. We can note that only after 8 hours we can get a good solution - about 40 production days, between 15 and 35% of the tasks performed in internal production centers and downtime rate of internal production centers near to 18%.

We highlight that the genetic algorithm parameters were adjusted considering an execution time of 12 hours. A genetic algorithm (GA) that works with a large population takes longer to found a good solution than a GA with a small population. However, it explores a larger solution space, thus obtaining better solutions. If a smaller execution time is required for running the proposed method, we should adjust the GA parameters in order to find good quality solutions.

We can also see in Figures 11, 12 and 13 that the objectives "to minimize the makespan" and "to minimize the internal production centers downtime" are not conflicting, i.e., when the value of one objective has an improvement, the value of the other also tends to improve. The objective "to maximize the use of internal production centers" has conflict with the others objectives.

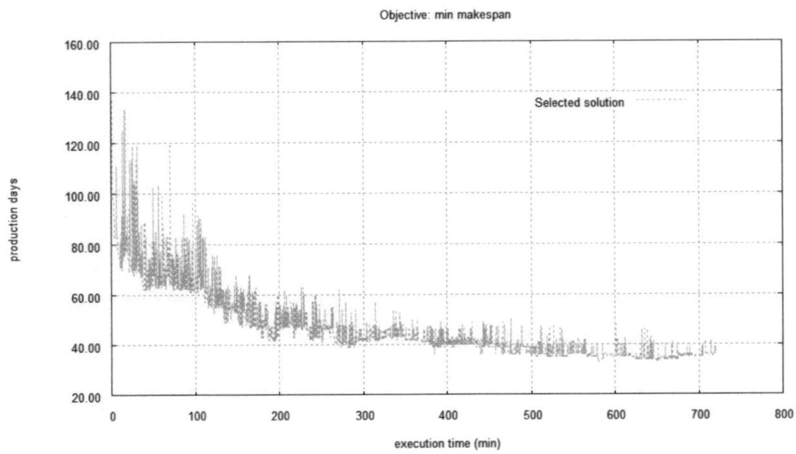

Figure 11. Selected solutions during 12 hours of execution. Objective: to minimize the makespan.

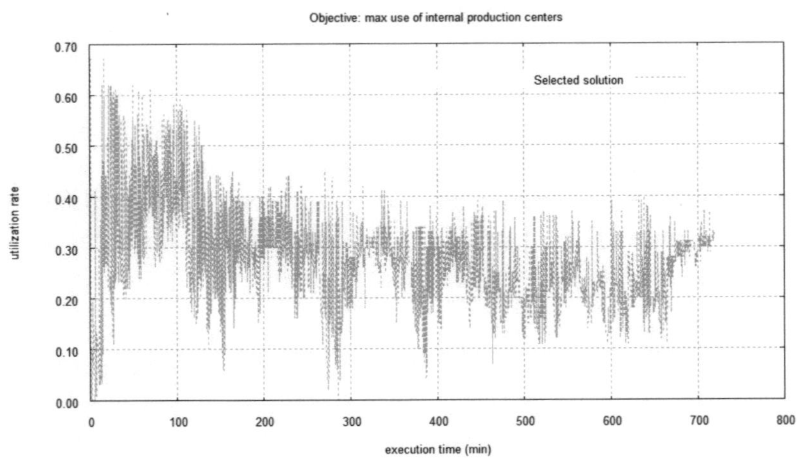

Figure 12. Selected solutions during 12 hours of execution. Objective: to maximize the use of internal production centers.

http://dx.doi.org/10.5772/53701

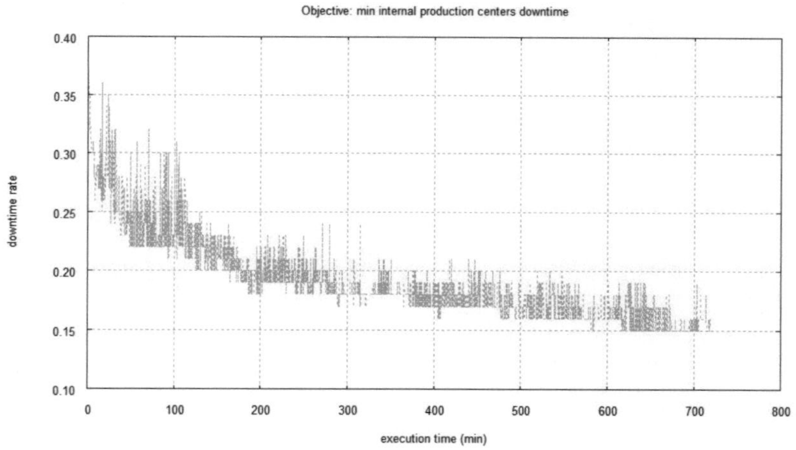

Figure 13. Selected solutions during 12 hours of execution. Objective: to minimize the internal production centers downtime.

Figure 14, 15 and 16 depict the obtained values for each selected solution and also for the best and worst solutions of the population at each generation. By analyzing the graphs presented in these figures, we can realize the diversification of the population throughout the generations. Again we can note that the objective "to maximize the use of internal production centers" (Figure 15) is conflicting with the other two. While the selected solutions tend to get close to the best solutions for the other two objectives (Figures 14 and 16), for this objective the selected solutions tend to get close to the worst solutions.

In the second experiment, the proposed method was compared with the commercial application PREACTOR, which is the leading software in the sector of finite capacity production planning in Brazil and worldwide, with over 4500 customers in 67 countries [26]. However, it was necessary to execute the proposed method considering only the objective "to minimize the makespan", because it was not possible to configure PREACTOR for working with three objectives.

Although the proposed method and PREACTOR perform the task scheduling, they have different purposes. PREACTOR is a universal tool of finite capacity production planning, which uses priority rules to perform the scheduling. The users of this tool can interact with the generated production planning. The proposed method is specific for garment companies, in which the large number of tasks makes difficult a manual evaluation. The purpose of the comparison between these methods is to validate the scheduling obtained by our proposal.

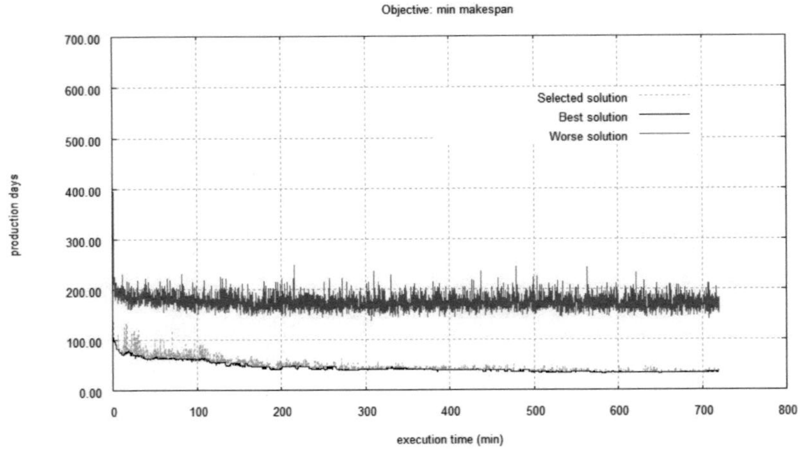

Figure 14. Best, worst and selected solutions during 12 hours of execution. Objective: to minimize the makespan.

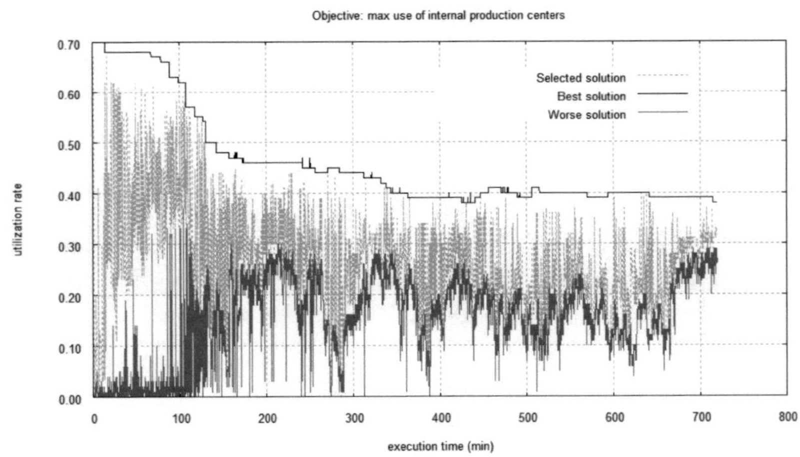

Figure 15. Best, worst and selected solutions during 12 hours of execution. Objective: to maximize the use of internal production centers.

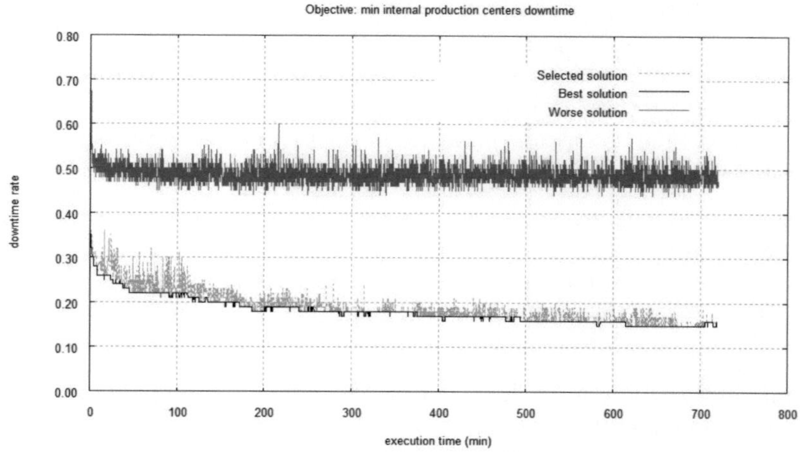

Figure 16. Best, worst and selected solutions during 12 hours of execution. Objective: to minimize the internal production centers downtime.

In this experiment, five runs of the proposed method were done. After 12 hours of execution, the proposed method has obtained an average of 32 days production planning, 17.9% lower than the 39 days production planning proposed by PREACTOR. The worst result obtained by the proposed method was 33 days production planning. It is worth to mention that PREACTOR took 12 minutes to reach its result. Figure 17 depicts that the proposed method overcomes the result obtained by PREACTOR after about 100 minutes of execution.

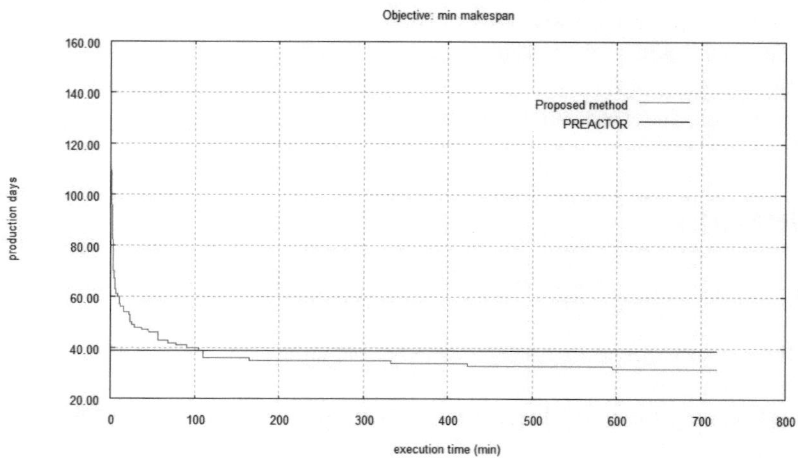

Figure 17. Proposed method × PREACTOR.

5. Conclusion remarks

The objective of this work is to develop a method to carry out the production scheduling of a Brazilian garment company in real time. Three objectives were considered: to minimize the total production time; to maximize the use of internal production centers; and to reduce the downtime of the internal production centers.

To achieve this goal, initially we have defined a mixed integer programming model for the addressed problem. Based on this model, we have proposed a method that combines a NSGA-II multiobjective genetic algorithm with the multicriteria method Weighted Sum Model - WSM. The mathematical model, the multiobjective genetic algorithm developed and its automatic combination with the multicriteria method WSM are contributions of this work.

Computational experiments were done in order to evaluate the proposed method. It was used real data provided by the analyzed garment company, which are related to May 2012 production demand. In the first experiment, the average results obtained by the proposed method were compared with the results manually obtained by the analyzed company at May 2011. Even with the increase of the production between these periods, the proposed method has decreased of 16.3% the production days. It has also got a higher rate of use and a smaller downtime rate of internal production centers. We have highlighted that the proposed method can obtain good quality solutions even when a smaller execution time is available. However, it is necessary to make an adjustment of the genetic algorithm parameters considering the available execution time.

In the second experiment, the proposed method was compared with the commercial software PREACTOR, considering only the objective "to minimize the makespan". The average obtained result was 17.9% better than the one obtained by PREACTOR. It was also shown that the proposed method overcame the result obtained by PREACTOR after about 100 minutes of execution.

It is worth to mention another advantage of the proposed method: as it is based on NSGA-II model, we can easily add and remove objectives. To do that a slight modification in the procedure that evaluates solutions is necessary. Thus, the proposed method can be suited to new needs of the garment industry or to other industrial branches.

Author details

Dalessandro Soares Vianna[1*], Igor Carlos Pulini[2] and Carlos Bazilio Martins[3]

*Address all correspondence to: dalessandrosoares@yahoo.com.br

1 Fluminense Federal University, Department of Computation – RCM, Rio das Ostras, RJ, Brazil

2 Candido Mendes University, Candido Mendes Research Center – CEPECAM, Campos dos Goytacazes, RJ, Brazil

3 Fluminense Federal University, Department of Computation – RCM, Rio das Ostras, RJ, Brazil

References

[1] C. M. Vigna and D. I. Miyake, "Capacitação das operações internas para a customização em massa: estudos de caso em indústrias brasileiras (in portuguese)", Produto & Produção, Bd. 10, Nr. 3, pp. 29--44, outubro 2009.

[2] D. F. Tubino, Planejamento e Controle da Produção (in portuguese), 2nd Edition, Atlas, 2009.

[3] R. Lindem, Algoritmos genéticos: uma importante ferramenta da inteligência computacional (in portuguese), 2nd Edition, Rio de Janeiro: Brasport, 2008.

[4] K. Deb, Multiobjective optimization using evolutionary algorithms, John Wiley & Son, 2008.

[5] J. E. C. Arroyo, P. S. Vieira and D. S. Vianna, "A GRASP algorithm for the multi-criteria minimum spanning tree problem", Annals of Operations Research, V. 159, pp. 125-133, 2008.

[6] M. Ehrgott and X. Gandibleux, "A survey and annotated bibliography of multiobjective combinatorial optimization", OR Spektrum, V. 22, pp. 425-460, 2000.

[7] D. S. Vianna, J. E. C. Arroyo, P. S. Vieira and R. R. Azeredo, "Parallel strategies for a multi-criteria GRASP algorithm", Produção (São Paulo), V. 17, pp. 1--12, 2007.

[8] D. F. Jones, S. K. Mirrazavi and M. Tamiz., "Multi-objective metaheuristics: An overview of the current state-of-art", European Journal of Operational Research, V. 137, pp. 1-19, 2002.

[9] E. Triantaphyllou, Multi-criteria decision making: a comparative study, Dordrecht: Kluwer Academic Publishers (now Springer), 2000.

[10] M. L. Pinedo, Scheduling: Theory, Algorithms, and Systems, 3rd Edition, Springer, 2008.

[11] P. Senthilkumar and S. Narayanan, "GA Based Heuristic to Minimize Makespan in Single Machine Scheduling Problem with Uniform Parallel Machines", Intelligent Information Management, V. 3, pp. 204-214, 2011.

[12] B. Santosa, M. A. Budiman and S. E. Wiratino, "A Cross Entropy-Genetic Algorithm for m-Machines No-Wait Job-Shop Scheduling Problem", Journal of Intelligent Learning Systems and Applications, V. 3, pp. 171-180, 2011.

[13] T. F. Abdelmaguid, "Representations in Genetic Algorithm for the Job Shop Scheduling Problem: A Computational Study", Journal Software Engineering & Applications, V. 3, pp. 1155-1162, 2010.

[14] L. Dayou, Y. Pu and Y. Ji, "Development Of A Multiobjective GA For Advanced Planning And Scheduling Problem", The International Journal of Advanced Manufacturing Technology, V. 42, pp. 974-992, 2009.

[15] W. S. Chang and C. C. Chyu, "A Multi-Criteria Decision Making for the Unrelated Parallel Machines Scheduling Problem", Journal Software Engineering & Applications, pp. 323-329, 2009.

[16] I. S. Franco, "Algoritmos híbridos para a resolução do problema de job shop flexível (in portuguese)", Master Thesis. Universidade Candido Mendes, Campos dos Goytcazes, RJ - Brazil, 2010.

[17] K. Deb, A. Pratap, S. Agarwal and T. Meyarivan, "A Fast and Elitist Multiobjective Genetic Algorithm: NSGA II", IEEE Transactions on Evolutionary Computation, V. 6, N. 2, pp. 182-197, April 2002.

[18] M. Köksalan, J. Wallenius and S. Zionts, Multiple Criteria Decision Making: From Early History to the 21st Century, Singapore: World Scientific, 2011.

[19] J. E. C. Arroyo, "Heurísticas e Metaheurísticas para Otimização Combinatória Multiobjetivo (in portuguese)", PhD Thesis, UNICAMP, SP - Brazil, 2003.

[20] A. S. Pitombeira-Neto, "Modelo híbrido de otimização multiobjetivo para formação de células de manufatura (in portuguese)", PhD Thesis, USP-São Carlos, SP - Brazil, 2011.

[21] H. Zhang and M. Gen, Effective Genetic Approach for Optimizing Advanced Planning and Scheduling in Flexible Manufacturing System, Seatle, 2006.

[22] Y. Li and Y. Chen, "A Genetic Algorithm for Job-Shop Scheduling", Journal Of Software, V. 5, pp. 269-274, 2010.

[23] A. Okamoto, M. Gen and M. Sugawara, "Robust Scheduling for APS using Multobjective Hybrid Genetic Algorithm", in proceedings of Asia Pacific Industrial Engineering and Management Systems Conference, Bangkok, Thailand, 2006.

[24] Z. Michalewicz, Genetic Algorithms + Data Structures = Evolution Programs, Springer, 1998.

[25] L. M. C. Dias, L. M. A. T. Almeida and J. Clímaco, Apoio multicritério à decisão (in portuguese), Coimbra: Universidade de Coimbra, 1996.

[26] TECMARAM, "Soluções para o gerenciamento de sistemas de produção (in portuguese", [Online]. Available: http://www.tecmaran.com.br. [Acessed at 04/08/2012].

[27] M. R. Garey and D. S. Johnson, Computers and Intractability: A Guide to the Theory of NP-completeness, San Francisco: W. H. Freeman, 1979.

[28] M. R. R. Olazar, "Algoritmos Evolucionários Multiobjetivo para Alinhamento Múltiplo de Sequências Biológicas (in portuguese)", PhD Thesis, UFRJ, RJ - Brazil, 2007.

Chapter 2

Grasp and Path Relinking to Solve the Problem of Selecting Efficient Work Teams

Fernando Sandoya and Ricardo Aceves

Additional information is available at the end of the chapter

http://dx.doi.org/10.5772/53700

1. Introduction

The process of selecting objects, activities, people, projects, resources, etc. is one of the activities that is frequently realized by human beings with some objective, and based on one or more criteria: economical, space, emotional, political, etc. For example, as a daily experience people should select what means of transportation and routes to utilize to arrive at a determined destination according to the price, duration of the trip, etc. In these cases, one must select the best subset of elements based on a large set of possibilities, the best in some sense, and in many cases there is an interest in the selected elements not appearing amongst themselves, if not it is better that they have different characteristics so that they can represent the existing diversity in the collection of original possibilities. Of course at this level people make these decisions intuitively, but commonsense, generally, is not a good advisor with problems that require optimized decision-making, and simple procedures that apparently offer effective solutions lead to bad decisions, thus this can be avoided by applying mathematical models that can guarantee obtainable effective solutions. In other human activities the selection of this subset has economic implications that involve a selection of a more diverse subset, a crucial decision, and difficult to obtain, which requires a correct process of optimization guided by a methodical form.

In the Operations Research literature, the maximum diversity problem (MDP) can be formulated by the following manner: If $V=\{1,\ 2,\ \cdots,\ n\}$ is the original set, and M is the selected subset, $M \subset V$, the search for optimizing the objective is as follows:

$$Max\ f_1(M)=div(M) \tag{1}$$

In the equation (1) the objective function $div(M)$ represents the measurement that has been made of the diversity in the subset selected. There are some existing models to achieve this goal, as well as a number of practical applications, as reported in [1, 2, 3, 4, 5]; in particular, we target the Max-Mean dispersion model in which the average distance between the selected elements is maximized, this way not only is there a search for the maximization of diversity, if not also the equitable selected set, also, the number of elements selected are as well a decision variable, as mentioned in [6].

Traditionally the MDP has permitted the resolution of concrete problems of great interest, for example: the localization of mutually competitive logistic facilities, for illustration see [3], composition of the panels of judges, [7], location of dangerous facilities, [1], new drugs design [8], formulation of immigration policies and admissions [9].

In the past, a great part of the public's interest in diversity was centered around themes such as justice and representation. On the other hand, lately there has been a growing interest in the exploitation of the benefits of diversity. Recently, in [6], it a potential case of the application of the selection of efficient work teams is mentioned. In practice, there are many examples when the diversity in a group enhances the group's ability to solve problems, and thus, leads to more efficient teams, firms, schools. For this reason, efforts have begun on behalf of the investigators to identify how to take advantage of the diversity in human organizations, beginning with the role played by the diversity in groups of people, for example in [10], Page *et al.* introduces a general work plan showing a model of the functionality of the problem solving done by diverse groups. In this scenario, it is determined that the experts in solving problems possess different forms of presenting the problem and their own algorithms that they utilize to find their solutions. This focus can be used to establish a relative result in the composition of an efficient team within a company. In the study it is determined that in the selection of a team to solve problems based in a population of intelligent agents, a team of selected agents at random surpasses a team composed by the best suited agents. This result is based on the intuition that when an initial group of problem solvers becomes larger, the agents of a greater capability will arrive to a similar conclusion, getting stuck in local optimum, and its greater individual capacity is more than uncompensated by the lack of diversity.

This chapter is organized in the following manner, beginning with the Section 2 study of concepts relating to diversity, and how it can be measured. Later on, in Section 4 we are introduced to the classic Maximum Diversity Problem, with differing variants, and the new problem Max-Mean, with which we attempted to resolve the first objective described by the equation (1), also revised are the formulations of the mathematical programming for these problems, and its properties are explored. In Section 5 an algorithm is developed based on GRASP with path relinking in which the local search is developed mainly with the methodology based on Variable neighborhood search, in Section 4 there is a documented extensive computerized experimentation.

2. Distances, similarities, and diversity

2.1. Definitions

Similarities are understood to be a resemblance between people and things. Although it is common to accept that diversity is an opposite concept of similarities, both terms perform within different structures, since similarities are a local function for each pair of elements. In contrast, diversity is a characteristic associated to a set of elements, which is calculated with the function of the dissimilarities within all the possible pairings. Where dissimilarities are the exact opposite of the similarities.

To be even more specific, to measure the diversity in M, $div(M)$, it is required to first have a clear definition of the connection, distance, or dissimilarity between each pair $i,\ j \in M$. The estimation of this distance depends on the concrete problem that is being analyzed, in particular in complex systems like social groups a fundamental operation is the assessment of the similarities between each individual pair. Many measurements of the similarities that are proposed in the literature, in many cases show similarities that are assessed as a distance in some space with adequate characteristics, generally in a metric space, as for example the Euclidian distance. In the majority of applications each element is supposed to able to be represented by a collection of attributes, and defining x_{ik} as the value of the attribute k of the element i, then, for example, utilizing the Euclidian distance:

$$d_{ij} = \sqrt{\sum_k (x_{ik} - x_{jk})^2}$$

Under this model, d, satisfies the axioms of a metric, although the empirical observation of attractions and differences between individuals forces abandoning these axioms, since they obligate an unnecessary rigid system with properties that can not adapt adequately the frame of work of this investigation: the measurements of similarities

In the literature, one can find the different measurements of similarities that can be applied to groups of people. For example, in [11] it is established that "the measurements of similarities of the cosine is a popular measurement of the similarities". On the other hand, in [10] it is established that the measurement of dissimilarities to treat the problem of the relation between the diversity and the productivity of groups of people can be established to solve problems. These measurements are developed in section 1.2. In [6] a similar measurement is utilized to solve a real case.

2.2. Similarity measurements

Given two individuals $i,\ j$ with the characteristics $x_i = (x_{i1},\ x_{i2},\ \ldots,\ x_{ip})$, $x_j = (x_{j1},\ x_{j2},\ \ldots,\ x_{jp})$ is defined by the measurement of similarities of the Cosine like:

$$d_{ij} = \frac{\sum_{k=1}^{p} x_{ik} x_{jk}}{\sqrt{\sum_{k=1}^{p} x_{ik}^2} \sqrt{\sum_{k=1}^{p} x_{jk}^2}} \quad (2)$$

On the other hand, in [10] the authors explain the problem with how diversity presents a group can increase the efficiency to solve problems, in particular in its investigation that authors use the following measurement of dissimilarities:

$$d_{ij}=\frac{\sum_{l=1}^{p}\delta(x_{il},\ x_{jl})}{p} \quad (3)$$

Where:

$$\delta(x_{il},\ x_{jl})=\begin{cases} -1 & si\ x_{il}=x_{jl} \\ |x_{il}-x_{jl}| & si\ x_{il}\neq x_{jl} \end{cases}$$

This measurement will take a negative value (in the case of similarities) and positives (in the case of dissimilarities). In general terms, we are referring to a d_{ij} as the dissimilarities or the distance between i and j.

2.3. Equity, diversity, and dispersion

The growing interest in the treatment of diversity also has originated in an effort to study the management of fairness, that is to say that all the practices and processes utilized in the organizations to guarantee a just and fair treatment of individuals and institutions. Speaking in general terms, the fair treatment is that which has or has exhibited fairness, being terms that are synonyms: just, objective, or impartial. Many authors, like French, in [12] the argument is that equality has to do with justice, for example the distribution of resources or of installations or public service infrastructures, and in the same manner the achievement of equality in diversity has been identified within as a problem of selection and distribution. Synthesized, one can say that the equality represents an argument concerning the willingness for justice, understanding this as a complicated pattern of decisions, actions, and results in which each element engages as a member of the subset given.

The other sub problem that should be resolved is how to measure diversity. Given a set $V=\{1,\ 2,\ \cdots,\ n\}$, and a measure of dissimilarity d_{ij} defined between every pair of elements of V, and a subset $M\subset V$, different forms have been established as their measure of diversity.

2.4. The measure of dispersion of the sum

With this calculated measurement of diversity and a subset as the sum of the dissimilarities between all the pairs of their elements; this is to say, the diversity of a subset M is calculated with the equation (4):

$$div(M)=\sum_{i<j,i,j\in M} d_{ij} \quad (4)$$

2.5. The measurement of dispersion of the minimum distance

In this case of the diversity of a subset given the establishment of how the minimum of these types of dissimilarities between the pairs of elements of the set; this is to say, like in equation (5).

$$div(M) = \min_{i<j, i,j \in M} d_{ij} \tag{5}$$

This type of measurement can be useful with contexts that can make very close undesirable elements, and thereby having a minimum distance that is great is important.

2.6. The measurement of the average dispersion

For a subset M, the average diversity is calculated by the expression of the equation (6)

$$div(M) = \frac{\sum_{i<j, i,j \in M} d_{ij}}{|M|} \tag{6}$$

Notice that this measurement of diversity is intimately associated with the measurement of the dispersion of the sum, that constitutes the numerator of the equation (6). In the literature lately some references have appeared in which the diversity is measured in this manner, for example in [13], in the context of systems Case-based reasoning, CBR, the authors defined the diversity of the subset of some cases, like the average dissimilarity between all the pairs of cases considered. So much so that in [6] diversity of a subset is defined by the equation (6) within the context of the models of the dispersion equation.

3. The maximum diversity problem

Once determined how to resolve the sub problem of estimating the existence of diversity in a set, the following is establishing the problem of optimizing what to look for the determined subset with maximum diversity. Such problem is named in the literature as The Maximum Diversity Problem.

The most studied model probably is the Problem in which it maximizes the sum of the distances or dissimilarities between the elements selected, this is to say the maximum measure of diversity of the sum established in the equation (4). In the literature there is also the problem also known with other denominations, as the Max-Sum problem [14], the Maximum Dispersion problem [15], Maximum Edge Weight Clique problem, [16], the Maximum edge-weighted subgraph problem, [18], or the Dense k-subgraph problem, [19].

Recently another model has been proposed in the context of equitative dispersion models [20], this model is denominated as the Maximum Mean Dispersion Problem (Max-Mean), that is the problem of optimization that consists in maximizing the equation (6), and one of the principal characteristics, that makes is different than the rest of the models of diversity, being that the number of elements selected also is a decision variable.

3.1. Formulations & mathematical programming models

Given a set $V=\{1,\ 2,\ \cdots,\ n\}$, and the dissimilarity relation d_{ij}, the problem is selecting a subset $M \subset V$, of cardinality $m<n$, of maximum diversity:

$$\max_{M \subset V} f_1(M)=div(M) \tag{7}$$

The manner in which diversity is measured in the equation (7) permits constructing the formulations of the different maximum diversity problems.

3.2. The Max-Sum problem

The Max-Sum problem consists in selecting the subset that has the maximum diversity, measuring the agreement of the equation (4):

$$\max_{M \subset V,\ |M|=m} \sum_{i<j, i, j \in M} d_{ij}$$

Introducing the binary variables: $x_i = \begin{cases} 1 \text{ if element } i \text{ is selected} \\ 0 \text{ otherwise} \end{cases} ;1 \le i \le n$

Therefore, this problem can be formulated as a problem of quadratic binary programming:

$$\max \sum_{i=1}^{n-1} \sum_{j=i+1}^{n} d_{ij} x_i x_j \tag{8}$$

$$s.t.\ \sum_{i=1}^{n} x_i = m \tag{9}$$

$$x_i \in \{0,1\};\ 1 \le i \le n \tag{10}$$

3.3. The Max-Mean problem

This problem can be described as:

$$\max_{M \subset V,\ |M| \ge 2} \frac{\sum_{i<j, i, j \in M} d_{ij}}{|M|}$$

Generically speaking, this problem deals with the maximization of the average diversity. A formulation of the mathematical programming with the binary variables is then:

http://dx.doi.org/10.5772/53700

$$\max \frac{\sum_{i=1}^{n-1} \sum_{j=i+1}^{n} d_{ij} x_i x_j}{\sum_{i=1}^{n} x_i} \tag{11}$$

$$s.t. \quad \sum_{i=1}^{n} x_i \geq 2 \tag{12}$$

$$x_i \in \{0,1\}, \quad 1 \leq i \leq n \tag{13}$$

In this problem the objective function (11) is the average of the sum of the distances between the selected elements, the constraint (12) indicates that at least two elements should be selected. Just as presented in [20], this is a fractional binary optimization problem, but can be linearized utilizing new binary variables, this way the problem is formulated for the equations (14) to (19):

$$\max \sum_{i=1}^{n-1} \sum_{j=i+1}^{n} d_{ij} z_{ij} \tag{14}$$

$$s.t. \quad y - z_i \leq 1 - x_i; \; z_i \leq y; \; z_i \leq x_i; \; z_i \geq 0; \; 1 \leq i \leq n \tag{15}$$

$$y - z_{ij} \leq 2 - x_i - x_j; \; z_{ij} \leq y; \; z_{ij} \leq x_i; \; z_{ij} \leq x_j; \; z_{ij} \geq 0; \; 1 \leq i < j \leq n \tag{16}$$

$$\sum_{i=1}^{n} x_i \geq 2 \tag{17}$$

$$\sum_{i=1}^{n} z_i = 1 \tag{18}$$

$$x_i \in \{0,1\}; \; 1 \leq i \leq n \tag{19}$$

Notice that the Max-Mean problem cannot be resolved applying a solution method for any of the other problems, unless applied repeatedly for all the possible values of $m = |M|; m = 2, \; 3, \; \ldots, \; n$. Surprisingly, as seen in Section 4, to find the solution of the Max-Mean problem with exact methods through resolving $(n - 1)$ Max-Sum problems requires much less time that resolves directly the formulation (14)-(19).

3.4. Computational complexity

This is known as the Max-Sum problem it is strongly NP-hard, as demonstrated in [9]. Recently, it has also been demonstrated in [20] that the Max-Mean problem is strongly NP-hard if the measurements of dissimilarities take a positive value and negative. Here the property 3 is demonstrated, this then indicates that if d_{ij} satisfying the properties of a metric, then the diversity $div(M)$ for any $M \subset V$ is always less than $div(M \cup \{k\})$ for any $k \notin M$, then, a solution with $m<n$ elements cannot be optimal in the Max-Mean problem, from there the optimum of this case is selecting all the elements.

Property 1 [12]

The Max-Sum Problem is Strongly NP-hard.

Property 2 [6]:

If the dissimilarity coefficients d_{ij} does not have restrictions in the sign, then the Max-Mean problem is strongly NP-hard.

Property 3:

The Max-Mean problem has a trivial solution $M = V$, if the dissimilarity measure is a metric.

Proof:

The Max-Mean problem consists in selecting a subset M such that $div(M)$ is maximized. Demonstrating that given the instance in which the dissimilarities are not negative, symmetrical, and satisfy the triangular inequality, the solution to the Max-Mean problem is selecting all the elements, that is to say: $M = V$.

For all $i,\ j \in M$ and $k \notin M$ the triangular inequality establishes that $d_{ij} \leq d_{ik} + d_{jk}$

Adding over all the possible pairs of elements in M:

$$\sum_{\substack{i,j \in M \\ i<j}} d_{ij} \leq \sum_{\substack{i,j \in M \\ i<j}} (d_{ik} + d_{jk})$$

But the right side of the last expression is equivalent to $(|M| - 1)$ times $\sum_{i \in M} d_{ik}$,

If representing with $m = |M|$, then:

$$\sum_{\substack{i,j \in M \\ i<j}} d_{ij} \leq \sum_{\substack{i,j \in M \\ i<j}} (d_{ik} + d_{jk}) = (m - 1) \sum_{i \in M} d_{ik} < m \sum_{i \in M} d_{ik}$$

Divided by m on has:

$$\frac{1}{m} \sum_{\substack{i,j \in M \\ i<j}} d_{ij} < \sum_{i \in M} d_{ik}$$

Adding the term $\sum_{\substack{i,j \in M \\ i<j}} d_{ij}$ on both sides of the last inequality:

$$\frac{m+1}{m} \sum_{\substack{i,j \in M \\ i<j}} d_{ij} < \sum_{\substack{i,j \in M \\ i<j}} d_{ij} + \sum_{i \in M} d_{ik} = \sum_{\substack{i,j \in M \cup \{k\} \\ i<j}} d_{ij}$$

Finally dividing for $(m+1)$:

$$div(M) = \frac{1}{m} \sum_{\substack{i,j \in M \\ i<j}} d_{ij} < \frac{1}{m+1} \sum_{\substack{i,j \in M \cup \{k\} \\ i<j}} d_{ij} = div(M \cup \{k\})$$

4. An efficient method to solve the Max-Mean problem

4.1. Exact solution for the MIP formulation

It is evident that an optimal solution can be obtained for the Max-Mean problem in an indirect manner if resolving the Max-Sum model for all the possible values of m; meaning, for $m = 2, \ 3, \ \ldots, \ n$, and then dividing the remaining solutions for the corresponding value of m. Then, the best value of these $(n - 1)$ values is the optimal Max-Mean model. Therefore, if $Z^*_{Max\text{-}Sum(m)}$ is the optimal value of the objective function of the Max-Sum problem with m selected elements, and $Z^*_{Max\text{-}Mean}$ is the optimal value of the Max-Mean problem, then:

$$Z^*_{Max\text{-}Mean} = \max_{m \in \{2,\ldots,n\}} \left\{ \frac{Z^*_{Max\text{-}Sum(m)}}{m} \right\}$$

This research takes into account two new types of test instances:

- Type I: This set contains 60 matrices of sizes: $n = 20, \ 25, \ 30, \ 35, \ 150 \ and \ 500$ with random numbers in $[-1,1]$ generated from a uniform distribution.
- Type II: There are also 60 symmetrical matrices, with $n = 20, \ 25, \ 30, \ 35, \ 150 \ and \ 500$, but with coefficients that generate with random numbers with a uniform distribution in $[-1, \ -0.5] \cup [0.5,1]$.

These test instances are found as available in the web site of the project OPTSICOM, [21].

Figure 1 shows the result of the resolution of the Max-Mean problem in an indirect way, for the test instances of type I and type II, of size $n = 30$, solving in an exact manner in each example 29 Max-Sum problems, each one of the cuadratic binary formulation (8)-(10). In this investigation, the Max-Sum problems are solved by the method of dynamic search using Cplex 12.4.0, the professional solver for mixed integer linear programming problems. Progress in computer technology and in design of MIP efficient algorithms and their implementation in Cplex 12.4.0 together with mathematical advance lead in some cases to satisfactory solution times. Unfortunately the MIP formulation described above cannot be solved in reasonable times for medium or large problems.

Also, Figure 1 shows that the Max-Mean value of the Max-Sum solution increases as m increases from 2 to certain value, and then this value decreases in the rest of the range. We have observed the same pattern (approximately a concave function) in all the examples tested with positive and negative distances randomly generated. We will consider this pattern to design an efficient GRASP algorithm.

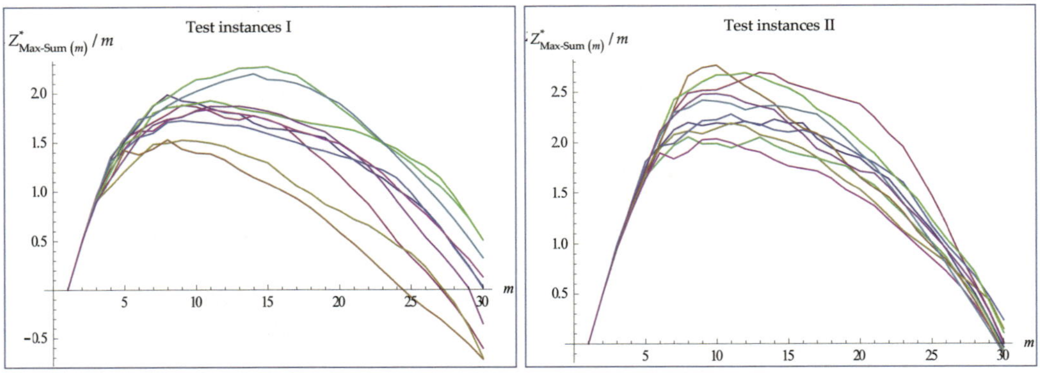

Figure 1. Evolution of the Optimal Values of the Max-Sum Problem divided for *m* value

Table 1 shows, that for each method and for each size of a problem, the average value of the objective function (*Value*) in the optimal solution, the average number of elements that end up being selected in the optimal solution (m), and the average time in seconds (CPU), ND signifies that the value is not available because the solution was not reached in 5 hours. Cplex 12.4.0 only permitted solving small problems in moderate times. In particular in the linear formulation (14)-(19) can only be resolved in test instances of $n<30$, and for $n=30$ the solution could not be obtained in a 5 hour process. Experiments with Cplex corroborate the difficulties that commercial branch-and-bound codes encounter when approaching the Max-Sum and Max-Mean problem with this manner.

		TYPE I		TYPE II	
n		**Max-Mean**	**Max-Sum (n-1) times**	**Max-Mean**	**Max-Sum (n-1) times**
20	***CPU (s)***	50.334	14.662	66.714	19.164
	Value	1.443	1.443	1.898	1.898
	m	7.400	7.400	7.500	7.500
25	***CPU (s)***	694.606	41.826	1995.100	59.581
	Value	1.732	1.732	2.207	2.207
	m	9.800	9.800	9.600	9.600
30	***CPU (s)***	> 5 horas	102.303	> 5 horas	182.176
	Value	ND	1.875	ND	2.383
	m	ND	10.700	ND	10.800

Table 1. Max-Mean Problem Solutions obtained with Cplex 12.4.0

Surprisingly, the Max-Sum model applied $(n - 1)$ times permits resolving instances of a greater size in less time, and one could obtain the solution for $n=30$ in 102.30 seconds on average, and for $n=35$ in 719.51 seconds in the type I problems, in the type II problems this requires more time. Yet, in instances of size $n=50$ in 5 hours cannot obtain the optimum solution for this strategy.

It can be concluded that if one desires to resolve the Max-Mean problem in an exact manner it is preferable to use the strategy to solve $(n - 1)$ times the Max-Sum model since the it consistently worked in much less time in all the experiments. This could be due to the fact that the relaxation continues in the Max-Sum problem providing better levels than the relaxation provided by the continued Max-Mean problem.

Given that the problems of the maximum diversity are NP-hard, it is clear that is required to make a heuristic design to resolve problems of large and medium size. In [6] a algorithm is developed based in GRASP that exploits the characteristics of the Max-Mean problem, and that is hybridized with other successful techniques of intensification, like Path Relinking (PR), and Variable Neighborhood Search, (VNS). This algorithm has resulted as an efficient solution to the medium and large problems.

4.2. Solving the Max-Mean problem

In this section, we describe a heuristic developing in [6] to solve the Max-Mean problem. This heuristic consists of a phase of construction GRASP, with a local search phase based on the Variable Neighborhood Search methodology subsequently it is improved with incorporation of a phase of post processing, based on Path Relinking.

4.3. GRASP construction phase

From the results shown in Figure 1, we can design a new constructive method in which we add elements to the partial solution under construction as long as the Max-Mean value improves, and when this value starts to decrease, we stop the construction. In this way, the method selects by itself the value of m, which seems adequate to this problem.

In place of a typical GRASP construction for diversity in which, first, each candidate element is evaluated by a greedy function to construct the Restricted Candidate List (RCL) and then an element is selected at random from RCL we utilizing an alternative design, in accordance with the proposed in recent studies [22] in which we first apply the randomization and then the greediness can obtain improved outcomes. In particular, in our constructive method for the Max-mean problem, we first randomly choose candidates and then evaluate each candidate according to the greedy function, selecting the best candidate, permitting better results.

More so specifically, given a partial solution M_k with k selected elements, the list of candidates CL is formed by the $(n - k)$ unselected elements. The list of restricted candidates, RCL, contains a fraction $\alpha (0<\alpha<1)$ of the elements of CL selected randomly, where α where is a parameter that should be selected adequately, generally by computational experiments.

Then, for each element $i \in RCL$, the method computes its contribution, $eval(i)$, if it is added to M_k to obtain $M_k \cup \{i\}$:

$$eval(i) = div(M_k \cup \{i\}) - div(M_k)$$

Where $div(\bullet)$ is the mean diversity defined in the equation (6).

Afterwards, the method selects the best candidate i^* in RCL if this improves the actual partial solution; this is to say, if $eval(i^*)>0$, and add it to the partial solution, $M_{k+1}=M_k \cup \{i^*\}$; otherwise, if $eval(i^*)\leq 0$, the method stops.

Figure 2 show the pseudo-code of this phase of construction of the method that one calls heuristic GRASP.

---

1. Select an element i^* at random in $N = \{1, 2, \ldots, n\}$.
2. Make $M_1 = \{i^*\}$, $k = 1$ and $improve = 1$.

While ($improve = 1$)

3. Compute $CL = \{1, 2, \ldots, n\} \setminus M_k$
4. Construct RCL with $\alpha|CL|$ elements randomly selected in CL
5. Compute $eval(i) = dm(M_k \cup \{i\}) - dm(M_k) \forall i \in RCL$
6. Select the element i^* in RCL with maximum $eval$ value

If $(eval(i^*) > 0)$

7. $M_{k+1} = M_k \cup \{i^*\}$
8. $k = k + 1$

Else

9. $improve = 0$

Figure 2. GRASP construction phase

4.4. Local search in GRASP

The GRASP construction usually does not obtain a local optimum and it is customary in GRASP to apply a local search method to the solution constructed. As shown in [6], previous local search methods for diversity problems limit themselves to exchange a selected with an unselected element, keeping constant the number m of selected elements. Since we do not have this size constraint in the Max-Mean model and we admit solutions with any value of m, we can consider an extended neighborhood based on the Variable Neighborhood Descent (VND) methodology.

We consider the combination of three neighborhoods in our local search procedure:

- N_1: Remove an element from the current solution, thus reducing the number of selected elements by one unit.

- N_2: Exchange a selected element with an unselected one, keeping constant the number of selected elements.
- N_3: Add an unselected element to the set of selected elements, thus increasing its size by one unit.

The order of exploration of the neighborhoods is given to try, in the range of possibility, diminishing the number of selected elements, increasing its diversity as well, which happens when a better solution is obtained in N_1. If this is not possible, one can conserve the cardinality of the selected set with the obligation of increasing diversity, just like what happens when exploring the neighborhood N_2. Finally, by exploring N_3, one is willing to increase the cardinality of the set selected if increasing diversity.

More specifically: Given a solution, M_m, the local search first tries to obtain a solution in N_1 to improve it. If it succeeds, and finds M'_{m-1} with $dm(M'_{m-1})>dm(M_m)$, then we apply the move and consider M'_{m-1} as the current solution. Otherwise, the method resorts to N_2 and searches for the first exchange that improves M_m. If it succeeds, and finds M'_m with $dm(M'_m)>dm(M_m)$, then we apply the move and consider M'_m as the current solution. In any case, regardless that we found the improved solution in N_1 or in N_2, in the next iteration the method starts scanning N_1 to improve the current solution. If neither N_1 nor N_2 is able to contain a solution better than the current solution, we finally resort to N_3. If the method succeeds, finding M'_{m+1} with $dm(M'_{m+1})>dm(M_m)$, then we apply the move and consider M'_{m+1} as the current solution (and come back to N_1 in the next iteration). Otherwise, since none of the neighborhoods contain a solution better that the current one, the method stops.

To accelerate the search in these neighborhoods, one would not make the exploration in a sequential manner over the elements of a specific neighborhood, if not one would evaluate the potential contribution to the partial solution of the following manner: Given a solution M_m, one calculates the contribution of each element selected i, just like the potential contribution of each element unselected i like:

$$d_s(i, M_m)=\sum_{j\in M_m} d_{ij}$$

Thus, when exploring N_1 one searches for the elements selected in the given order by d_s, where the element with the smallest value is tested first. Similarly, when exploring N_2 proving the selected elements in the same order but the elements unselected in the inverse order, this is to say, first considering the elements not selected with a grand potential contribution to the partial solution.

Finally, when exploring N_3 the elements not selected, that are considered to be added in the actual solution, they are explored in the same manner than in N_2, in which the element with the largest contribution is considered first. Figure 3 outlines the pseudo-code of this phase.

1. Select an element i^* at random in $N = \{1, 2, ..., n\}$.
2. Make $M_1 = \{i^*\}$, $k = 1$ and $improve = 1$.

While ($improve = 1$)

3. Compute $CL = \{1, 2, ..., n\} \setminus M_k$
4. Construct RCL with $\alpha|CL|$ elements randomly selected in CL
5. Compute $eval(i) = dm(M_k \cup \{i\}) - dm(M_k) \forall i \in RCL$
6. Select the element i^* in RCL with maximum $eval$ value

If ($eval(i^*) > 0$)

7. $M_{k+1} = M_k \cup \{i^*\}$
8. $k = k + 1$

Else

9. $improve = 0$

Figure 3. Local search in GRASP

4.5. GRASP with path relinking

The Path Relinking algorithm was described for the first time in the framework of tabu search method, it operates on a Elite Set of solutions (ES), constructed with the application of a previous method. Here we apply GRASP to build ES considering both quality and diversity. Initially ES is empty, and we apply GRASP for $b = |ES|$ iterations and populate it with the solutions obtained (ordering the solutions in ES from the best x^1 to the worst x^b). Then, in the following GRASP iterations, we test whether the generated solution x', qualify or not to enter ES. Specifically, if x' is better than x^1, it enters in the set. Moreover, if it is better than x^b and it is sufficiently different from the other solutions in the set ($d(x', ES) \geq dth$), it also enters ES. To keep the size of ES constant and equal to b, when we add a solution to this set, we remove another one. To maintain the quality and the diversity, we remove the closest solution to x' in ES among those worse than it in value.

Given two solutions, x ,y , interpreted as binary vectors with n variables, where variable x_i takes the value 1 if element i is selected, 0 otherwise, the distance $d(x, y)$ can be computed as $d(x, y) = \sum_{i=1}^{n} |x_i - y_i|$ and the distance between a solution x' and the set ES, $d(x', ES)$, can be computed as the sum of the distances between x' and all the elements in ES.

The path relinking procedure $PR(x, y)$ starts with the first solution x, called the initiating solution, and gradually transforms it into the final one y called the guiding solution. At each iteration we consider to remove an elements in x not present in y, or to add an element in y not present in x. The method selects the best one among these candidates, creating the first intermediate solution, $x(1)$. Then, we consider to remove an element in $x(1)$ not present in y, or to add an element in y not present in $x(1)$. The best of these candidates is the second in-

http://dx.doi.org/10.5772/53700

termediate solution $x(2)$. In this way we generate a path of intermediate solutions until we reach y. The output of the PR algorithm is the best solution, different from x and y, found in the path. We submit this best solution to the improvement method. Figure 4 shows a pseudo-code of the entire GRASP with Path Relinking algorithm in which we can see that we apply both $PR(x, y)$ and $PR(y, x)$ to all the pairs x, y in the elite set ES.

```
1. Set GlobalIter equal to the number of global iterations.
2. Apply the GRASP method (construction plus improvement)
 for b=|ES| iterations to populate ES={ x^1, x^2, ..., x^b }.
3. iter=b+1.
While( iter≤GlobalIter )
  4. Apply the construction phase of GRASP ⇒ x.
           5. Apply the local search phase of GRASP to x⇒ x'.
  If ( f(x') >f(x^1)  or  (f(x') >f(x^b) and d(x',ES) ≥ dth ) )
               6. Let x^k be the closest solution to x' in ES with f(x')>f(x^k).
               7. Add x' to ES and remove x^k.
               8. Update the order in ES (from the best x^1 to the worst x^b).
9. Let x^best= x^1.
For(i=1 to b-1 and j=i+1 to b)
           10. Apply PR(x^i,x^j) and PR(x^j,x^i), let x be the best solution found
           11. Apply the local search phase of GRASP to x⇒ x'.
           If(f(x') >f(x^best))
                     12. x^best= x'.
13. Return x^best.
```

Figure 4. GRASP with Path Relinking

4.6. Comparison with existing methods

We also propose a new adaptation of existing methods for several models of maximum diversity problem.

Prokopyev et al. in [20] introduced several models to deal with the equitable dispersion problem and the maximum diversity problem. The authors proposed a GRASP with local search for the Max-MinSum variant in which for each selected element (in M), they compute the sum of the distances to the other selected elements (also in M) and then calculate the minimum of these values. The objective of the Max-MinSum model is to maximize this minimum sum of distances. We can adapt the method above, originally proposed for the Max-MinSum, to the Max Mean model. We call this adapted method GRASP1.

Also, Duarte and Martí in [26] proposed different heuristics for the Max-Sum model. In particular the authors adapted the GRASP methodology to maximize the sum of the distances among the selected elements. We also adapt this algorithm to solve the Max-Mean Model, and we call the entire method (constructive phase + local search) GRASP2.

Adaptation details of these algorithms can be seen in [6]

In the final experiment we target the 20 largest instances in our data set (n=500). Table 3 shows the average results on each type of instances of GRASP1, GRASP2 and our two methods, GRASP and GRASP with Path Relinking described in this Section. Results in Table 3 are in line with the results obtained in the previous experiments. They confirm that GRASP consistently obtains better results than GRASP1 and GRASP2. As shown in the last column of Table 3, Path Relinking is able to improve the results of GRASP in all the instances.

5. Numeric experiments with test instances

This section contains the results of a large number of numerical experiments that is made to evaluate and calibrate the GRASP algorithm, which was implemented in Mathematica V.7[1], the experiments are processed in an Intel Core 2 Laptop, 1.4 GHz and 2GB de RAM. The parameters of the algorithms were calibrated through extensive computational experiments.

5.1. GRASP heuristic performance on small problems

In this section a comparison is made of the performance of the heuristic GRASP and the exact optimal reported for small problems. The results are shown in Table 2.

Small instances of size $n=30$ were used, the largest are for those that can be resolved with Cplex 12.4.0 in an exact manner in reasonable times. Since the optimal is known, a measurement of the precision of the methods is the difference in relative percentage with respect to the optimum (GAP). Table 2 shows the average of the objective function (Value), the average number of elements selected (m), the times that the optimum was reached (# of optimal times), the relative difference with the optimal (GAP) and the average time in seconds (CPU Time).

		GRASP constructive	**Cplex 12.4.0**
Type I	Value	1.87351	1.874955
	m	10.8	10.7
	# optimal times	9	10
	GAP	0.084%	0%
	CPU Time	0.35444	102.303
Type II	Value	2.377163	2.383
	m	10.3	10.8
	# optimal times	6	10
	GAP	0.397%	0%
	CPU Time	0.3444	182.176

Table 2. Performance of the constructive phase in small problems

1 Mathematica is a computational software program used in scientific, engineering, and mathematical fields and other areas of technical computing. It is developed by Wolfram Research.

Only applying the constructive phase of GRASP one can reach the exact optimum of the problems 90% of the times, for the test instances of type I, and the 80% of the times in the test instances of type II, and in a reduced amount of time (less than a second), also in instances in which the optimum is not found, the GAP is very small.

5.2. Solution to large problems

Being that is no longer possible to compare the optimal solution of these problems, in place of GAP it is reported that a percentage of deviation in respect to the best solutions found in the experiments, the represented value in the tables like deviation, and that it is equal to:

$$Deviation = \frac{best\ solution\ -\ current\ solution}{best\ solution} \times 100\%$$

		GRASP	GRASP+PR	GRASP1	GRASP2
Type I	Value	7.71370	7.7977	6.6796	7.0163
	m	139.4	145.2	154.4	157.6
	# Best	0	10	0	0
	Deviation	1.07%	0.00%	14.31%	10.01%
	CPU (sec.)	717.3	688.1	1414.5	950.9
Type II	Vaue	10.2957	10.437	88.98	92.68
	m	143.2	144.4	186.1	170.4
	# Best	0	10	0	0
	Deviation	1.53%	0.00%	14.74%	11.18%
	CPU (sec.)	662.422	679.641	804.8	708.3

Table 3. Comparison of the obtained results with GRASP+PR in large instances

Table 3 shows that the Path Relinking phase permitted improvements to the results of the heuristic GRASP, GRASP1 (based in [20]) and GRASP2 (based in [26]) in all of the test instances of size $n = 500$ and for the two types of examples considered

5.3. Search profile in Variable Neighborhood Search (VNS) methodology by GRASP

Our local search in the heuristic GRASP utilizes three types of neighborhoods, generated according to the methodology VNS, these neighborhoods are represented by: N_1 (remove an element from the solution), N_2 (exchange a selected element with an unselected one), and N_3 (add an unselected element to the solution). This way an interesting study is measured by the contribution of each type of neighborhood to the quality of the final solution.

Figure 6 depicts a bar chart with the average number of times, in the 20 instances of size $n = 150$ used in our preliminary experimentation, that each neighborhood is able to improve the current solution. We can see that, although N_2 improves the solutions in a larger number of cases, N_1 and N_3 are also able to improve them and therefore contribute to obtain the final solution.

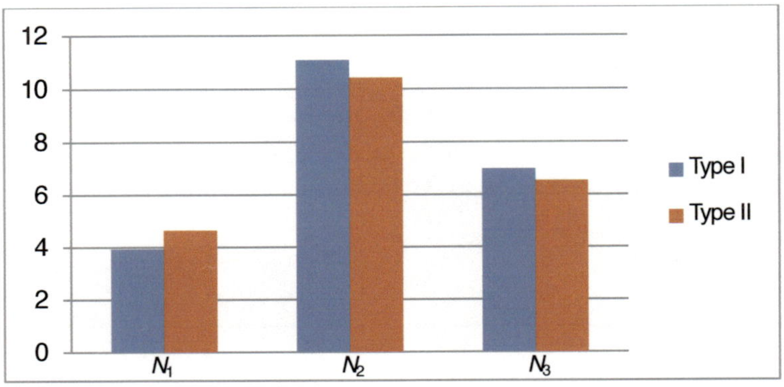

Figure 5. Average number of improvements of each GRASP neighborhood

Curiously, if one calculates the was average contribution to the improvement of the function of the objective that provides the exploration in each one of the types of neighborhoods, one can observe that the neighborhoods of type N_1 and N_3 provide greatest contribution on average compared with the visit to the neighborhood N_2, as shown in Figure 6.

5.4. Solution of large problems using GRASP with Path Relinking

In this section the experiments made are described with the 20 test instances of size $n=500$. Table 3 shows the summary of the results obtained in the large instances when applying the algorithms proposed, the values correspond to the achieved averages with each one of the test instances of this size.

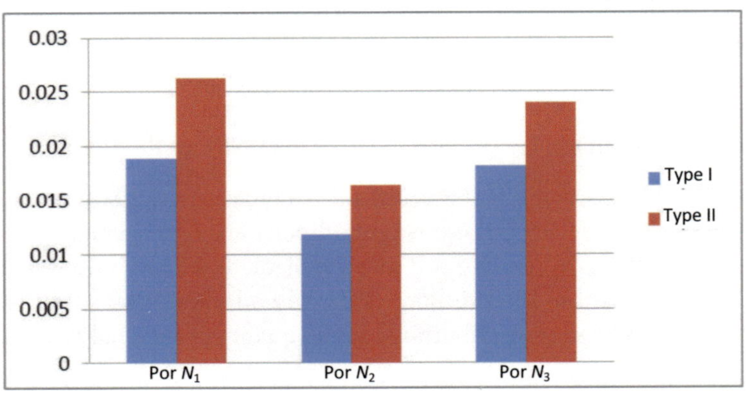

Figure 6. Contribution to improving the objective function value for each neighborhood

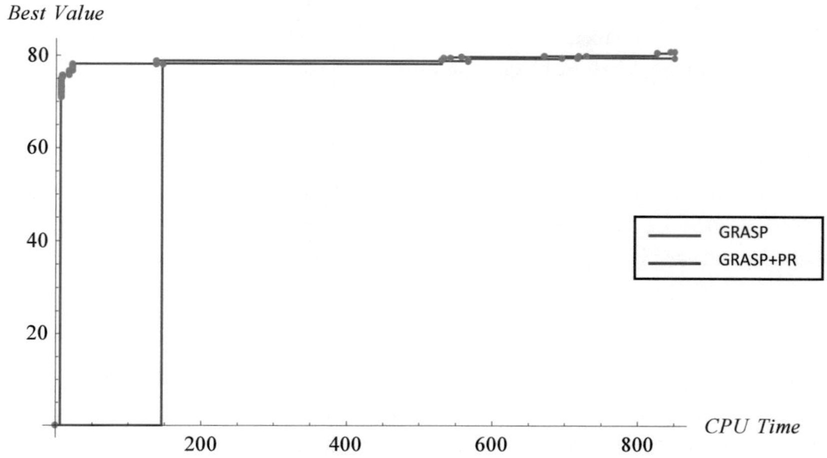

Figure 7. Search profile of GRASP and GRASP+PR

5.5. Search profile

Finally, to complete the analysis of the comparison of the efficiency of the algorithms that are designed, graphs were made of the profile of search of the algorithms; this is to say, since these heuristics were improving the value of the objective function of the time of execution. In Figure 7 one can observe the amplified details of its profile for a search in the neighborhood of the best values found. The figure clearly shows the GRASP achieves good solutions quickly. The execution of GRASP+PR, the phase of relinking of trajectories is executed after the elite set, *ES*, has been populated, which occurs after approximately 450 seconds, on average. Then the phase of path relinking properly said, by applying the procedure to each pair of solutions of the elite set, the evolution of the best solution found show that this phase permits obtaining the best solutions quickly, surpassing the GRASP (without PR), that after a certain moment does no achieve improvements in the solutions in the same proportion that GRASP+PR, and therefore is seen surpassing due to this. Similar profiles are observed for Type II instances

6. A case of application for the Max-Mean problem

6.1. Teams that are more diverse are more efficient for problem solving than those less diverse

This way, in daily activities of organizations, companies, schools, sport teams, etc. it has been observed through evidence that diversity has an important role on the ability for groups of people to solve problems. Lately, literature investigations have shown formally that this empirical phenomenon is true, proportioning a theoretic justification for this fact, for example in [10]. A consequence of this is that, under certain circumstances, the groups of people that have conformed in a diverse manner can surpass the productivity of the groups conformed by the people individually more capable to resolve these problems; meaning, in a certain way diversity triumphant over the ability.

From a practical point of view, this result implies that, for example, a company that wants to conform a team should not look for simply a selection of individuals with a greater qualification for it, probably the most efficient selection would be to choose a diverse group. In reality the ideal would be that the groups of work be conformed by people with great qualifications and diversity; yet, these two objectives tend to be opposing one another since the diversity of the team formed by the people more qualified tends to be smaller, as demonstrated in [24].

The idea in the background is that we have a population of capable people to realize any task; these people have different levels of ability or of productivity for resolve it, and if one must select the work teams of this population for realizing a task, one can consider two possible groups: in the first only individuals are chosen with high qualifications, and in the second "diverse" individuals are chosen in some sense It turns out that the first finish in some way arriving to the same solution, creating a more difficult and confusing work for each other, on the other hand the second group the diversity created more perspectives and thus more opportunity of avoiding a halt on the search for a solution of the problems, generating in some way the right environment to increase the individual productivity of each one, and therefore of all groups. From a formal point of view what happens in the first group, under certain hypothesis, the people that are highly qualified tend to convert into similar points of view and ways to solve problems from which the set of optimal locations that the group can reach is reduced. Although the second group of diverse members originates a set of optimal locations more widely, and thus has more opportunities to improve.

6.2. Diversity in identity and functional diversity, perspectives and heuristics

In terms of a population, understood as "diversity in identity", or simply "diversity," to the differences en its demographic characteristics, cultural, ethnics, academic formation, and work experience. On the other hand, "formal diversity" is known as the differences in how these people focus and treat problem solving. An important fact is that these two types of diversity are correlated, since it has been identified experimentally a strong correlation between two types of diversity, just as demonstrated in [25]. Given the connection, it can be deduced that diverse groups in identity are functionally diverse.

In the literature, the focus was employed on a person to resolve a problem is a representation or an encoding of the problem in its internal language, and it can be known as "perspective." Formally, a perspective P is a mapping of the set of solutions of a problem into the internal language of the person resolving a problem.

On the other hand, the way in which people attempt to resolve a problem, or how they look for solutions are known as "heuristic." Formally, a heuristic is a mapping H of the encoding of the solutions in an internal language of the person that will solve the problem into the solutions set. This way, given a particular solution, the subset generated by the mapping H is the set of the other solutions that the person considers. In this manner, the ability to resolve the problem on behalf of a person is represented by its couple of perspective-heuristic (P, H). Two people can differ in one of these components or in both; meaning, they can have different perspectives or different heuristics, or differ on both. A solution would be the local optimum for a person if and only if when the person encodes the problem and applies the heuristic, neither of the other solutions that the person considers has the abilities, and thus will have a few optimal locales, causing the group to become stuck with one of the solutions.

6.3. How to select the most productive work team

From an intuitive point of view, the conclusion that diverse groups in identity can surpass groups that are not diverse (homogeneous) due to its grand functional diversity based on the affirmation, well reception, that if the agents inside of the groups have equal individual ability to solve problems, a functional diverse group surpasses a homogeneous group. In [24] it has demonstrated that groups with functional diversity tend to surpass the best individual agents being that the agents in the group have the same ability. This still leaves open an important question: Can a functionally diverse group, whose members have less individual ability, have a superior performance than the group of people that have more abilities individually? In [10] finally resolves in a affirmative manner this question, making a mathematical demonstration to this fact. Even though certain doubts still surge in a natural manner in respect to: How many members should this group have in such a way that the average diversity within the group be at its maximum?, and, can one detect which is the group more functionally diverse?

This way, if considering the actual situation in which an Institution desires to hire people to solve a problem. To realize a good selection the Institution usually gives a test to the applicants, around 500, to estimate their abilities individually to solve a problem. Supposing that all the applicants are individually capable to solve them, then they have the formation and experience necessary, but have different levels of ability. It is doubtful if the Institution should hire:

i. The person with the highest score obtained on the test;

ii. The 10 people with the highest scores;

iii. 10 people selected randomly from the group of applicants;

iv. The 10 people most diverse in identity of the group of applicants;

v. The group of people most diverse on average of the group of applicants.

Ignoring the possible problems of the communication within the groups, the existing literature suggests that (ii) is better than (i), [25],since most people will be looking in a wider space, having then more opportunities to obtain better solutions, in place of the action of the person graded best that will stay stuck in one of the optimal locations. Recently in [10] it has been demonstrated formally that (iii) is better than (ii).

In this manner, the institution fails based on the group of people with the highest scores, meaning the most prepared individually, go on to form the best work team, and thus the company should hire (ii), since it is demonstrated as under certain hypothesis that (iii) is a better decision, as seen in [10]. The authors have come to determine that a team of people selected randomly have more functional diversity and under certain conditions surpass the performance of (ii). since under the set of conditions identified by the authors, the functional diversity of a group of the people that are individually capable to resolve the problem necessarily becomes smaller, which in the end, the advantage of having best abilities individually is seen as more than compensated by the greater diversity of the randomly selected group.

Figure 8 shows a scheme of the problem of selecting a team, and the options considered.

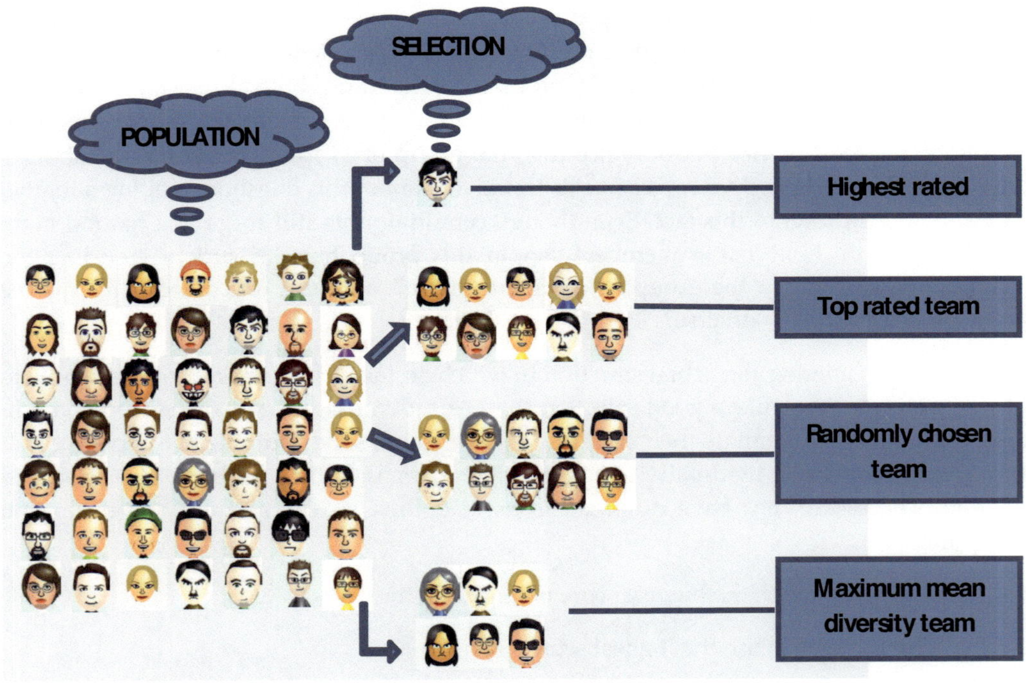

Figure 8. As the institution should hire?

Notice that the authors in the proof do not even use the equipment with the maximum diversity, if not a randomly selected group, and even then are able to demonstrate that it is better, thanks to the greater diversity inherent in the random group next to the group with the most abilities individually. Here we prove in the corollary of the theorem 2, that if selecting the group with more diversity on average, this is to say hire the group formed according to (iv), this would result more productive than hiring than that formed randomly (iii), and,

http://dx.doi.org/10.5772/53700

by transitivity, better than the group formed by the best scores (ii) and lastly better than simply choosing the best scored (i).

On the other hand, the literature says little or nothing at all about (v), since classically in the problems of diversity have considered the number of elements chosen as a given value, yet in the practice applications it is not clear how to choose the number of elements to be selected, and the best option would be to leave the process itself of optimization the one that demonstrates its value. This way, the focus of our analysis is centered on the dispute between the importance of the abilities of the individuals of each person in the group, their functional diversity (trapped by the diversity of identity), and the size of the ideal group.

A conclusion to all this is that the diversity in the organizations should be encouraged, which implies new policies, organizational forms, and styles of administration. In the context of solving a problem, the value of a person depends on their ability to improve the collective decision, since the contribution of this person depends in great measure to the perspectives and heuristics of the other people that make up the teamwork. The diversity in the focus of the solution of the problem in respect to the other people is an important predictor of its value, and in the end can be more relevant than its individual ability to solve the problem on its own. This was, to estimate the potential contribution of a person in teamwork, it is more important to make an emphasis in measuring how this person thinks differently, before estimating the magnitude of the ability of the person from aptitude tests or intelligence tests.

Although one has to be more conscious of some aspects that have not been considered and that can have influence in the performance of a team of people. For illustration, the groups with diversity in identity can often have more conflicts, more problems of communication, less mutual respect and less trust amongst the members of a homogeneous groups, which can create a diminishment of performance in diverse groups. In (16) it is mentioned that the people with similar perspectives but with diverse heuristics can communicate with one another without any problem, but people with diverse perspectives can have problems when comprehending the solutions identified by the other members of the group, in this sense the best of the organizations would be to find people with similar perspectives but guarantee a diversity of heuristics, in this manner, the organizations can exploit better the benefits of the diversity while minimizing the costs of the lack of communication.

6.4. Basics hypothesis and relationship between ability and diversity

In this section it is stated in theorem 1, demonstrated in [10], that explains the logic behind the fact that a team of people chosen at random, from a database of applicants that are capable to solve problems, it is better than the team formed by the people more individually capable, from there a result is established, that is immediate, being that the team of people with the most diversity surpasses the team formed by the people with the most abilities for solving problems.

To establish a theoretic result, consider the population from where the team will be selected, this is to say the applicants, represented with con Φ with to satisfy the following suppositions

- The applicants are trained to solve the problem. Given the initial solution, the applicants can find a better solution, even if it is only a little better;
- The problem is difficult, none of the applicants can find the optimal solution always;
- The applicants are diverse, and therefore for any potential solution that is not the optimal, at least one applicant can find the best solution;
- The best applicant is the only one.

If we consider a team of applicants chosen randomly from Φ to according to some distribution, the theorem establishes what, with probability 1, sample sizes N_1 and N exist, $N_1 < N$, just like in the collective performance of the team of the N_1 applicants chosen at random surpasses the collective performance of the N_1 best applicants.

To formulate the theorem 1 more precisely, consider X the solution set of the problem, a function that gives the value of each solution $V : X \rightarrow [0,1]$, supposing as well that Vit has the only maximum x^*, and that $V(x^*)=1$. Each applicant ϕ beings from the initial solution x and uses the search rule to find the maximum, but is not always found, if not generally gets stuck in a local optimum, if $\phi(x)$ is the local optimum when the applicant ϕ starts his search in x. This way $\phi(X)$ represents the local optimal set for the applicant ϕ.

Each applicant is characterized by the pair (ϕ, ν),), and an estimation of the performance as the value expected of the search by treating the solving of the problem, represented by $E(V;\phi, \nu)$; this is to say that,

$$E(V;\phi, \nu) = \sum_{x \in X} V(\phi(x))\nu(x)$$

The hypothesis should be satisfies by the applicants ϕ, with which the theorem is demonstrated through the following:

HYPOTHESIS 1 (Consistency):

i. $\forall x \in X : V(\phi(x)) \geq V(x)$

ii. $\forall x \in X : \phi(\phi(x)) = \phi(x)$

HYPOTHESIS 2 (Difficulty):

$\forall \phi \in \Phi, \exists x \in X : \phi(x) \neq x$

HYPOTHESIS 3 (Diversity):

$\forall x \in X \setminus \{x^*\}, \exists \phi \in \Phi : \phi(x) \neq x$

HYPOTHESIS 4 (Uniqueness):

arg max $\{E(V;\phi, \nu) : \phi \in \Phi\}$ is unique

Hypothesis 1 indicates that given the initial solution the people always try to find better solutions, but never select the worst solution, and get stuck in the optimal locale. Hypothesis 2 implies that no one, individually, can reach the optimum always from any point. In hypothesis 3, it is established in a simple manner that the essence of diversity, when a person is stuck in an local optimum always has someone that can find the best due to a different focus. Hypothesis 4 establishes that within the set of applicants considering that a better unique performance exists. With these hypotheses, the theorem 1 is proved in [10].

THEOREM 1: Being Φ a set of people that satisfy the hypothesis 1–4. And being μ his probability distribution. Then, with probability 1, positive integers N y N_1, $N > N_1$, just like the performance of the set of N_1 people selected at random surpasses the performance of the set of the N_1 individually more capable, taken from the group of N people independently chosen according to μ.

The theorem shows that a randomly selected group works better than a group formed for the better, is an immediate extender of the results as presented in the following corollary, which is demonstrated here, in which it is established more directly in relation between the diversity and ability.

COROLLARY: If Φ is a set of people that satisfy the hypothesis of the theorem 1, then, with probability 1, positive integers N and N_1, $N > N_1$ exist and that which the performance of the set of the group of N_1 people that maximize $\{div(M),\ M \subset \Phi,\ |M| = N_1\}$ exceeds the overall performance of the N_1 people individually more capable, taken of the group of N people independently chosen according to μ.

Proof:

The proof is immediate, since the theorem is based that the diversity of the set of people randomly selected is more diverse than the set of people with the most individual abilities. This way, if selecting the group of people most diverse, helps this surpass the performance of the group of people selected randomly, due to the major diversity of the first, and for theorem 1, this last group surpasses the performance of the group formed by the people with more abilities individually. It continues as transitivity the result that is shown in the corollary.

6.5. Resolution of a case study

Finally, we apply the method solving a real instance. In particular we apply them to obtain a diverse assembly of professors from a set of n=586 in the ESPOL University at Guayaquil (Ecuador). For each professor, we record 7 attributes (tenure position, gender, academic degree, research level, background, salary level, and department), and the similarity measure between each pair of them is computed with the modified difference measure described in the equation 3. The solution obtained with our GRASP+PR method in 127.1 seconds has 90 professors and a similarity value of 1.11. Table 4 it is shown that the results detailed and each one of the 10 trials.

TRIAL	GRASP+PR			GRASP		
	CPU time	Value	*m*	CPU time	Value	*m*
1	127.094	1.11542	101	116.631	1.09397	90
2	125.081	1.11393	100	113.7384	1.09487	96
3	120.028	1.10484	96	111.7161	1.07699	86
4	115.622	1.10311	92	113.4575	1.09058	88
5	114.616	1.10251	94	119.4957	1.09844	101
6	139.309	1.10811	96	126.6417	1.08316	95
7	123.162	1.12293	100	128.5092	1.03239	86
8	134.082	1.12600	100	119.378	1.05797	92
9	125.688	1.12033	101	109.6741	1.07982	97
10	134.566	1.11090	97	101.3805	1.05701	107
MEAN	**125.9248**	**1.11281**	**97.7**	**116.06222**	**1.07652**	**93.8**

Table 4. Average results about the 10 successive runs

7. Conclusions

The main result of this paper provides conditions under which, a diverse group of people will outperform a group of the best. Our result provides insights into the trade-off between diversity and ability. An ideal work team would contain high-ability problem solvers who are diverse.

According to our approach, the problem of designing the most efficient work team is equivalent to the maximum diversity problem, wich is a computationally difficult, In particular we study the solution of the Max-Mean model that arises in the context of equitable dispersion problems. It has served us well as test case for a few new search strategies that we are proposing. In particular, we tested a GRASP constructive algorithm based on a non-standard combination of greediness and randomization, a local search strategy based on the variable neighborhood descent methodology, which includes three different neighborhoods, and a path relinking post-processing.

We performed extensive computational experiments to first study the effect of changes in critical search elements and then to compare the efficiency of our proposal with previous solution procedures.

The principles of the proposed equity measure can be applied to solve the problem of selecting efficient work teams. Therefore, more research is necessary in this area, especially to solve the subproblem to measure diversity. The results from a comparative study carried out with the other algorithms favor the procedure that we proposed, also is able to solve large instances. The focus of our future research will be on the development of multi-objective optimization that attempts to balance efficiency or ability and diversity, namely a study on the selection of the best and most diverse, which gives a flexible and interactive way for decision makers to make the tradeoff between ability and diversity.

Author details

Fernando Sandoya[1*] and Ricardo Aceves[2*]

*Address all correspondence to: fsandoya@espol.edu.ec

1 Institute of Mathematics, Escuela Superior Politécnica del Litoral (ESPOL), Guayaquil, Ecuador

2 Facultad de Ingeniería, Departamento de Sistemas, Universidad Nacional Autónoma de México

References

[1] E. Ercut and S. Neuman, "Analytic Models for locating undesirable facilities," European Journal of Operational Research, vol. 40, pp. 275-291, 1989.

[2] F. Glover, C. Kuo, and K. S. Dhir, "A discrete optimization model for preserving biological diversity," Appl. Math. Modeling, vol. 19, pp. 696 - 701, 1995.

[3] F. Glover, C. C. Kuo, and K. Dhir, "Heuristic Algorithms for the Maximum Diversity Problem," Journal of Information and Optimization Sciences, vol. 19, no. 1, pp. 109 - 132, 1998.

[4] K. Katayama and H. Narihisa, "An Evolutionary Approach for the Maximum Diversity Problem," Studies in Fuzziness and Soft Computing, vol. 166, pp. 31-47, 2005.

[5] E. Erkut, "The discrete p-dispersion problem," European Journal of Operational Research, vol. 46, pp. 48-60, 1990.

[6] R. Martí and F. Sandoya, "GRASP and path relinking for the equitable dispersion problem," Computers and Operations Research, http://dx.doi.org/10.1016/j.cor.2012.04.005, 2012.

[7] M. Lozano, D. Molina, and C. García-Martínez, "Iterated greedy for the maximum diversity problem," European Journal of Operational Research, 2011.

[8] Thorsten Meinl, Maximum-Score Diversity Selection, primera ed.: Südwestdeutscher Verlag, 2010.

[9] M. Kuo, F. Glover, and K. Dhir, "Analyzing and modeling the maximum diversity problem by zero-one programming," Decision Sciences, no. 24, pp. 1171 - 1185, 1993.

[10] Scott Page and Lu Hong, "Groups of diverse problem solvers can outperform groups of high-ability problem solvers," PNAS, vol. 101, no. 46, pp. 16385 - 16389, 2004.

[11] T. Q. Lee and Y. T. Park, "A similarity Measure for Collaborative Filtering with Implicit Feedback," ICIC 2007, pp. 385-397, 2007.

[12] E. French, "The importance of strategic change in achieving equity in diversity," Strategic Change, vol. 14, pp. 35–44, 2005

[13] B. Smyth and P. McClave, "Similarity vs. Diversity," Lecture Notes in Computer Science, vol. 2080, pp. 347-361, 2001.

[14] J. Ghosh, "Computational aspects of the maximum diversity problem," Operations Research Letters, no. 19, pp. 175 - 181, 1996.

[15] J. Wang, Y. Zhou, J. Yin, and Y. Zhang, "Competitive Hopfield Network Combined With Estimation of Distribution for maximum DIversity Problems," IEEE Transactions on systems, man, and cybernetics, vol. 39, no. 4, pp. 1048-1065, 2009.

[16] B. Alidaee, F. Glover, G. Kochenberger, and H. Wang, "Solving the maximum edge weight clique problem via unconstrained quadratic programming," European Journal of Operational Research , no. 181, pp. 592 – 597, 2007.

[17] E. Macambira, "An application of tabu search heuristic for the maximum edge-weighted subgraph problem," Annals of Operational Research, vol. 117, pp. 175-190, 2002.

[18] U. Feige, G. Kortsarz, and D. Peleg, "The dense k-subgraph problem," Algorithmica, vol. 29, no. 3, pp. 410-421, 2001.

[19] O. Prokopyev, N. Kong, and D. Martínez-Torres, "The equitable dispersion problem," European Journal of Operational Research, no. 197, pp. 59 - 67, 2009.

[20] Opticom Project. (2012, Mayo) Opticom Project. [Online]. http://www.optsicom.es/

[21] M. Resende and R. Werneck, "A hybrid heuristic for the p-median problem," Journal of heuristics, vol. 10, no. 1, pp. 59-88, 2004.

[22] P. Hansen and N. Mladenovic, "Variable neighborhood search," in Handbook in Metaheuristics, F. Glover and G. Kochenberger, Eds., 2003, pp. 145-184.

[23] S. Page, The Difference: How the Power of Diversity Creates better Groups, Firms, Schools, and Societies. New Jersey: Princenton University Press, 2007.

[24] J. Polzer, L. Milton, and W. Swann, "Capitalizing on Diversity: Interpersonal Congruence in Small Work Groups," Administrative Science Quarterly, vol. 47, no. 2, pp. 296 - 324, 2002.

[25] Duarte A, Martí R. “Tabu Search and GRASP for the Maximum Diversity Problem”, European Journal of Operational Research; 178, 71-84, (2007)

Chapter 3

Meta-Heuristic Optimization Techniques and Its Applications in Robotics

Alejandra Cruz-Bernal

Additional information is available at the end of the chapter

http://dx.doi.org/10.5772/54460

1. Introduction

Robotics is the science of perceiving and manipulating the physical world. Perceive information on their envioronments through sensors, and manipulate through physical forces. To do diversity tasks, robots have tobe able to accomodate the ennormous uncertainty that exist in the physical world. The level of uncertainty depends on the application domain. In some robotics applications, such as assembly lines, humans can cleverly engineer the system so that uncertainty is only a marginal factor. In contrast, robots operating in residential homes, militar operates or on other planets will have to cope with substantial uncertainty. Managing uncertainty is possibly the most important step towards robust real-world robot system.

If considerate that, for reduce the uncertainty divide the problem in two problems, where is the first is to robot perception, and another, to planning and control. Likewise, path planning is an important issue in mobile robotics. It is to find a most reasonable collision-free path a mobile robot to move from a start location to a destination in an envioroment with obstacles. This path is commonly optimal in some aspect, such as distance or time. How to find a path meeting the need of such criterion and escaping from obstacles is the key problem in path planning.

Optimization techniques are search methods, where the goal is to find a solution to an optimization problem, such that a given quantity is optimized, possibly subject to a set of constraints. Modern optimization techniques start to demonstrate their power in dealing with hard optimization problems in robotics and automation such as manufacturing cells formation, robot motion planning, worker scheduling, cell assignment, vehicle routing problem, assembly line balancing, shortest sequence planning, sensor placement, unmanned-aerial vehicles (UAV) communication relaying and multirobot coordination to name just a few. By example, in particle, path planning it is a difficult task in robotics, as well as construct and control a robot. The main propose of path planning is find a specific route in order to reach the target destination.

Given an environment, where a mobile robot must determine a route in order to reach a target destination, we found the shortest path that this robot can follow. This goal is reach using bio-inspired techniques, as Ant Colony Optimization (ACO)and the Genetics Algorithms (GA).

A principal of these techniques, is by example, with a colony can solve problems unthinkable for individual ants, such as finding the shortest path to the best food source, allocating workers to different tasks, or defending a territory from neighbors. As individuals, ants might be tiny dummies, but as colonies they respond quickly and effectively to their environment. They do it with something called Swarm Intelligence.

These novel techniques are nature-inspired stochastic optimization methods that iteratively use random elements to transfer one candidate solution into a new, hopefully better, solution with regard to a given measure of quality.

We cannot expect them to find the best solution all the time, but expect them to find the good enough solutions or even the optimal solution most of the time, and more importantly, in a reasonably and practically short time. Modern meta-heuristic algorithms are almost guaranteed to work well for a wide rangeof tough optimization problems.

1.1. Previous work

Path planning is an essential task navigation and motion control of autonomous robot. This problem in mobile robotic is not simple, and the same is attached by two distint approaches. In the *classical approaches* present by Raja et al.[49]cited according to [3]the C-space, where the representation of the robot is a simple point. The same approach is described by Latombe's book [4]. Under concept of C-space, are developedpath planning approaches with roadmap and visibility graph was introduced[5].Sparce envioroments considering to polygonal obstacles and their edges [6, 7]. The Voroni diagram was introduced [8]. Other approach for roadmap andrecient applications in [9,10]. Cell descomposition approach [11, 12, 13, 14, 15,16]. A efficente use of grids [17].

A related problem is when both, the map and the vehicle position are not know. This problem is usually nown as Simultaneous Localization and Map Building (SLAM), and was originally introduced [18]. Until recently,have been significative advances in the solution of the SLAM problem [19,20,21,22].

Kalman filter methods can also be extended to perform simultaneous localization and map building. There have been several applications in mobile robotic, such as indoors, underwater and outdoors. The potential problems with SLAM algorithm have been the computational requeriments. The complexy of original algortihm is of $O(N^3)$ but, can be reduced to $O(N^2)$where, N will be the number of landmarks in the map [23].

In computational complexity theory, path planning is classified as an *NP* (nondeterministic polynomial time) complete problem [33]. *Evolutionary approaches* provide these solutions. Where, one of the high advantage of heuristic algorithms, is that it can produce an acceptable solution very quickly, which is especially used for solving *NP-complete problems*.

A first path planning approach of a mobile robot trated as non-deterministic polynomial time hard (*NP-hard*) problem is [31]. Moreover, even more complicated are the environment dynamic, the classic approaches to be incompetent [32]. Hence, evolutionary approaches such as Tabu Search (TS), Artificial Neural Network (ANN), Genetic Algorithm (GA), Particle Swarm Optimization (PSO), Ant Colony Optimization (ACO) and Simulated Annealing (SA), name a few, are employed to solve the path planning problem efficiently although not always optimal.

Genetic Algorithm (GA) based search and optimization techniques have recently found increasing use in machine learning, scheduling, pattern recognition, robot motion planning, image sensing and many other engineering applications. The first research of Robot Motion Planning (RMP), according to Masehian et al.[53] although GA, was first used in [42] and [43]. An approach for solution the problem of collision-free paths is presented in [44].GA was applied [45, 46, 48] in planning multi-path for 2D and 3D environment dimension and shortest path problem. A novel GA searching approach for dynamic constrained multicast routing is developed in [49]. Parallel GA [50], is used for search and constrained multi-objective optimization. Differentials optimization used hybrid GA, for path planning and shared-path protections has been extended in [51, 52]. In [62, 63, 64, 65], has been a compared of differential algorithms optimization GA (basically for dynamic environment), subjected to penalty function evaluation.

By other side, thetechnique PSO have some any advantages [35], such as simple implementationwith a few parameters to be adjusted. Binary PSO [37] withouta mutation operator[36]are used to optimize the shortest path. Planning in dynamic environment, that containing invalid paths (repair by a operator mutation), are subjected to penalty function evaluation [38]. Recently, [39] proposedwith multi-objective PSO and mutate operator path planning in dangerous dynamics environment.Finally, a newperspective global optimization is propossed [40].

Ant Colony Optimization (ACO) algorithms have been developed to mimic the behavior of real ants to provide heuristic solutions for optimization problems. It was first proposed by M. Dorigoin 1992 in his Ph. D. dissertation [54]. The first instance of the application of Ant Colony Optimization in Probabilistic Roadmap is the work [55, 56]. In [57] an optimal path planning for mobile robots based on intensified ACO algorithm is developed. Also in 2004, ACO was used to plan the best path [58]. ACRMP is presented in [60]. An articulated RMP using ACO is introduced in [59]. Also, a path planning based on ACO and distributed local navigation for multi robot systems is developed in [66]. Finally, an approach based on numerical Potential Fields (PF) and ACO is introduced in [61] to path planning in dynamic environment. In [66] a fast two-stage ACO algorithm for robotic path planning is used.

The notion of using Simulated Annealing (SA) for roadmap was initiated in [67]. PFapproach was integrated with SA to escape from local minimaand evaluation [68,70]. Estimates using SA for a multi-path arrival and path planning for mobile robotic based on PF, is introduced in [69, 72]. A path planning based on PF approach with SA is developed in [72].Finally, in [71] was presented a multi operator based SA approach for navigation in uncertain environments.

A case particle are militar applications, with an uninhabited combat air vehicle (UCAV). The techniques employed, have been proposed to solve this complicated multi-constrained optimization problem, solved contradiction between the global optimization and excessive information. Such techniques used to solution this problem are differential evolution [24], artificial bee colony [29], genetic algorithm [25], water drops optimization (chaotic and intelligent) [30] and ant colony optimization algorithm [26, 27, 28].

2. Robot navigation

2.1. Introduction

Mobile robots and manipulator robots are increasingly being employed in many automated envionments. Potential applications of mobile robots include a wide range such a service robots for elderly persons, automated guide vehicles for transferring goods in a factory, unmmaned bomb disposal robots and planet exploration robots. In all thes applications, the mobile robots perform their navegation task using the building blocks (see figure 1) [1], the same, is based on [2] known with the Deliberative Focus.

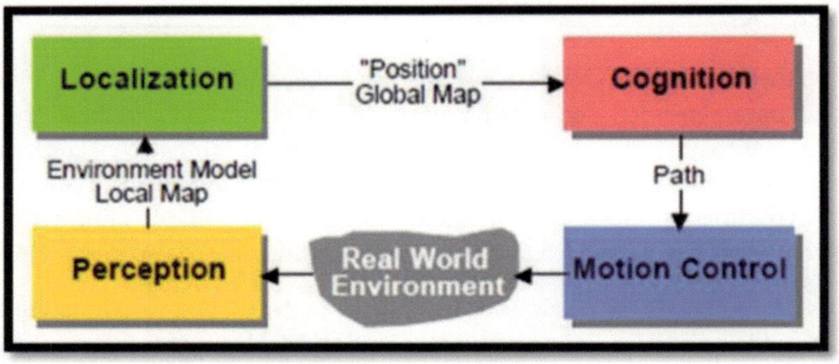

Figure 1. Deliberative Focus.

While perception of enviroment refers to understanding its sensory data, finding its pose or configuration in the surroundings is localization and map building. Planning the path in accordance with the task by using cognitive decision making is an essential phase before actually accomplishing the preferred trajectory by controlling the motion. As each of the building blocks is by itself a vast research field.

2.2. Map representation methods

When, Rencken in1993 [73] defined the map building problem as sensing capacity of robot, can be split in two, where robot know a pre-existing map or it has to build this, through information of the environment. According to above is assumed that the robot begins a exploration without having any knowledge of the environment, but with a exploration strategy, and it depends strongly on the kind of sensors used, the robot builds its own perception of environment[74].

http://dx.doi.org/10.5772/54460

A proposal of spatial representation is to sample discretely the two- or three-dimensional environment. This isa sample space in *cells* of a *uniform grid*for two-dimensional or considering the volume of elementsthat are used to represent objets named *voxel*.

Geometric maps are composed of the union of simple geometric primitives. Such maps are characterized by two key properties: the set of basic primitives used for describing objects, and the set of operators used to manipulate objects. The fundamentals problems with this technique are lack of stability, uniqueness, and potentiality.

Within the *geometric representations*, the *topological representation* can be used to solve abstract tasks that are not void reliance on error-prone metric, provided an explicit representation of connectivity between regions or objects. A topological representation is based on an abstraction of the environment in terms of discrete places (*landmarks*) with edges connecting them. In [76], present an example of this topological representation, where after of delimited region of interest, used a GA for the landmark search through the image.

2.3. Path planning

The basic path planning problem refers to determining a path in configuration space between an initial configuration (start pose) of the robot and a final configuration (finish pose). Therefore, several approaches for path planning exist of course a particular problem of application, as well as the kinematic constraints of the robot [77]. Although is neccesary make a serie of simplied with respect to real environment, the techniques for path planning can be group in *discrete state space* and *continuum space*.

To efficiently compute of search the path through techniques as A* [14] and Dynamic programming. The difference between them usually, resides in the simplicity to define or compute the evaluation function, which hardly depends on the nature of the environment and the specific problem.Other techniques for mapping a robot's environment inside a discrete searchable space include visibility graphs and Voronoi diagrams [75].

Path planning in a *continuum space* is consideret as the determination of an appropriate trajectory within this continuum. Two of the most known techniques for continuous state space are the potentialfields [61] and the vector field histogram methods. Alternatively,these algorithms, can be based on the *bug algorithm*[41], guaranteed to find a path from the beginning until target, if such path exists. Unfortunately, these methods can be generated arbitrarytrajectories worse than the optimal path to the target.

3. Population-based meta-heuristic optimization

Many results in the literature indicate that metaheuristics are the state-of-the-art techniques for problems for which there is non efficient algortihm. Thus, meta-heuristics approach approximationsallow solving complex optimization problems. Although these methods, cannot guarantee that the best solution found after termination criteria are satisfied or indeed its global optimal solution to the problem.

3.1. Optimization

The theory of optimization refers to the quantitative study of optima and the methods for finding them. Global Opitimization is the branch of applied mathematics and numerical analysis that focuses on well optimization. Of course T. Weise in [81], the goal of global optimization is to find to the best possible elements x* form a set X according to a set criteria $F = \{f_1, f_2, \ldots, f_n\}$These criteria are expressed as mathematical function, that so-called objetive functions. In the Weise's book[81] the Objective Function is described as:

DefinitionObjective Funcition. An objective funtion $f : X \mapsto Y$ with $Y \subseteq R$ is a mathematical function which is subject to optimization.

Global optimization comprises all techniques that can be used to find the best elements x* in X with respect to such criteria $f \in F$.

3.2. Nature-inspied meta-heuristic optimization

The high increase in the size of the search space and the need of proccesing in real-time has motivated recent researchs to solving scheduling problem using nature inspired heuristic techniques. The principal components of any metaheuristic algorithms are: intensification and diversification, or explotation and exploration. The optimal combination of these will usually ensure that a global optimization is achievable.

1. Initialize the solution vectors and all parameters.
2. Evaluate the candidate solutions.
3. Repeat
    a. Generation a new candidate solutions via the nature o social behaviors.
    b. Evaluate the new candidate solutions.
4. Until meet optimal criteria.

Figure 2. General Description for Nature Inspired Algorithm

3.3. Genetic algorithms

In essence, a Genetic Algorithm (GA) is a search method based on the abstraction Darwinian evolution and natural selection of biological systems and respresenting them in the mathematical operator: croosover or recombination, mutation, fitness, and selection of the fittest.

The application of GA to path planning problem requires development of a chromosome

representation of the path, appropriate constraint definition to minimize path distance, such that is providing smooth paths. It is assumed that the environment is static and known.

Cited according to [81], the genotypes are used in the reproduction operations whereas the values of the objective funtions f(or fitness function), where$f \in F$are computed on basis of the phenotypes in the problme space X which are obtained via the genotype-phenotype mapping (gpm) [82, 83, 84, 85], where G is a space any binary chain.

http://dx.doi.org/10.5772/54460

$$\forall g \in \mathsf{G}\ \exists x\ \in \mathsf{X}: gpm\ (g) = x \tag{1}$$

$$\forall g \in \mathsf{G}\ \exists x\ \in \mathsf{X}: P(gpm\ (g) = x) > 0 \tag{2}$$

1. Random Initial Population.
2. Repeat
   - a. Calculated through evaluation to aptitude of individual (gpm) of course (2).
   - b. Select two individuals, assign its aptitude probabilistic.
   - c. Applied Genetic Operators. Only two gene with best aptitude probabilistic.
     - i. Crossover to the couples.
     - ii. Mutation to the equal rate probabilistic.
   - d. Extinction (or null reproduction) by a poor aptitude probabilistic individual.
   - e. Reproduction.
3. Until finish condition

Figure 3. GA Modified.

3.4. Swarm intelligence

Swarm intelligence (SI) is based on the collective behavior. The collective behaviorthat emerges is a form of autocatalytic behaviour [34], self-organized systems. It's typically made up of a population of simple agents interacting locally with one another and with their environment. Natural examples of SI include ant colonies, bird flocking, animal herding, bacterial growth, and fish schooling. Nowadays swarm intelligence more generically, referes design complex adaptive systems.

3.4.1. Particle Swarm Optimization

Particle Swarm optimization (PSO), is a form of swarm intelligence, in which the behavior of a biological social systems. A particullaritied is when, looks for food, its individuals will spreadin the environment and move around independently. According to [81] Particle Swarm Optimization, a swarm of particles (individuals) in a n-dimensional search space G is simulated, where each particle q has a position genotype $p.g \in \mathsf{Q} \subseteq \mathrm{R}^n$ in this case n-dimensional is two, likewise a velocity $p.v \in \mathrm{R}^n$. Therefore, each particle p has a memory holding its best position (can be reference to minim distance Euclidian of target (p) respect to q) best (q) $\in \mathsf{G}$. In order to realize the social component, the particle furthermore knows a set of topological neighbors N(q) which could well be strong landmarks in the R^n.

This set could be defined to contain adjacent particles within a specific perimeter, using the Euclidian distance measure d_{euc} specified by

$$d_{euc} = \| p - q_i \|_2 = \sqrt{\sum_{i=1}^{n} (\mathbf{p} - q_{(x,y)})^2} \tag{3}$$

$$d_{p.g} = \min\{d_{euc}(p,\ q_i) \mid q_i \in \mathrm{Q}\} \tag{4}$$

$$p.v. = \omega \cdot v_i + \alpha \cdot rnd() \cdot (p_i - p.g) + \beta \cdot rnd() \cdot (g_{best} - p.g) \tag{5}$$

$$p.g = d_{p.g} + p.v. \tag{6}$$

3.4.2. *Ant Colony Optimization*

Ant Colony Optimization (ACO) has been formalized into a meta-heuristic for combinatorial optimization problems by Dorigo and co-workers [78], [79].This behavior, described by Deneubourg [80] enables ants to find shortest paths between food sources and their nest. While walking, they decide about a direction to go, they choose with higher probability paths that are marked by stronger pheromone concentrations.

ACO has risen sharply. In fact, several successful applications of ACO to a wide range of different discrete optimization problems are now available. The large majorities of these applications are to *NP-hard* problems; that is, to problems for which the best known algorithms that guarantee to identify an optimal solution have exponential time worst case complexity. The use of such algorithms is often infeasible in practice, and ACO algorithms can be useful for quickly finding high-quality solutions.

ACO algorithms are based on a parameterized probabilistic model the *pheromone model*, is used to model the chemical pheromone trails. Artificial ants incrementally construct solutions by adding opportunely defined solution components of the partial solutions in consideration. The first ACO algorithm proposed in the literature is called Ant System (AS) [56].

In the construction phase, an ant incrementally builds a solution by adding solution components to the partial solution constructed so far. The probabilistic choice of the next solution component to be added is done by means of transition probabilities, which in AS are determined by the following *state transition rule*:

$$\mathrm{P}(c_r|s_a[c_l]) = \begin{cases} \dfrac{[\eta_r]^{\alpha}[\tau_r]^{\beta}}{\sum_{c_u \in j(s_a[c_l])}[\eta_u]^{\alpha}[\tau_u]^{\beta}} & \text{if } c_r \in J(s_a[c_l]) \\ 0 & \text{otherwise} \end{cases} \tag{7}$$

Once all ants have constructed a solution, the *online delayed pheromone update rule* is applied:

$$\tau_j \leftarrow (1-\rho)\cdot\tau_j + \sum_{a \in A} \Delta\tau^{s_a}{}_j$$

where

$$\Delta\tau^{s_a}{}_j = \begin{cases} F(s_q) & \text{if } c_j \text{ is a component of } s_a \\ 0 & \text{otherwise} \end{cases} \tag{8}$$

http://dx.doi.org/10.5772/54460

This pheromone update rule leads to an increase of pheromone on solution components that have been found in high quality solutions.

4. Behavior fusion learning

4.1. Representation and initial population

Applied the performance and success of an evolutionary optimization approach given by a set of objective functions *F* and a problem space X is defined by:

- Its basic parameter settings like the population size $\leq ms$ or the crossover and mutation rates.
- Whether it uses an archive Arc of the best individuals found.
- The fitness assignment process and the selection algorithm.
- The genotype-phenotype mapping connecting the search Space and the problem space.

Such that:

- All ants begin in the same node. Applied (6) to node initiate.
- Initial population with a frequency *f*.
- L^+ is evaluated with a cost of T^+. This implies, that *j* is visited only once.
- The transition rule is (9).

4.2. Genetic operators and parameters

The properties of their crossover and mutatrion operations are well known and an extensive body of search on them is avaible [87, 88].

The natural selections is improved the next form:

- Select four members to population (two best explorers and two best workers).
- Applied crossover.
- The probability the mutation is same to the percentage this.
- Performed null reproduction.

A string chromosome can either be a fixed-length tuple (9) or a variable-length list (10).

$$\mathsf{G} = \forall \left(g[1],\ \ldots,\ g[n] : g[i] \in \mathsf{G}_i \forall_i \in 1 \ldots n \right) \tag{9}$$

$$\mathsf{G} = \{\forall\ lists(g : g[i] \in \mathsf{G}_T\ \ \forall\ 0 \leq i \leq len(g)\} \tag{10}$$

4.2.1. Selection

Elitist selection, returns the $k<ms$(number of individuals to be placed into the mating)best elements from the list. In general evolutionary algorithms, it should combined with a fitness assignment processs that incorporates diversity information in order to prevent premature convergence.The elitist selection, force to the best individuals, according with to fitness function, to move to the next iteration.

4.2.2. Crossover

Amongst all evolutionary algortihms, genetic algorithms have the recombination operation which probably comes closest to the natural paragon.

Example of a fixed-length string, applied to the best explorer and the best workers obtain the two best gene.

1. Init random value α, β and γ.
2. Repeat
   a. Applied mask.
   b. The value is one, pass to gen father.
   c. The value is cero, pass to gen mother.
3. Until ms.

Figure 4. Crossover Algorithm.

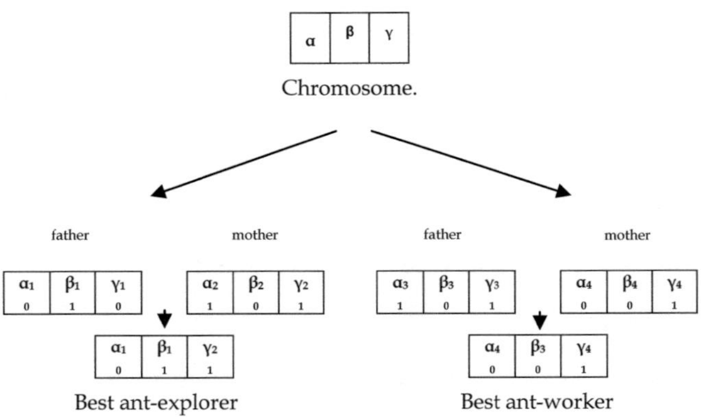

Figure 5. Example of Crossover, of course steps (b) and (c) crossover algorithm.

4.2.3. Mutation

The mutation operation applied, mutate $N \mapsto N$ is used to create a new genotype $g_n \in N$ by modifying an existing one. The way this modification is performed is application-dependent. It may happen in a randomized or in a deterministic fashion.

$$g_n = mutate(g) : g \in N \tag{11}$$

Therefore, the mutation performed only one of the three gene in the chromosome offspring. The selected gen must a change in his allele (inherited), by a new random value in the same.

4.2.4. Null reproduction or extinction

After the crossover of the mutation (if is the case) is need performed a null reproduction or extinction of the ant workers or ant explorer. This allows the creation of fixed-length strings individuals means simple to create a new tuple of the structure defined by the genome and initialize it with random values.

4.3. Path planning through evolutive ACO

The modifcation of the proposed ACO algorithm is applied. Due to in this modification have several parameters that determine the behavior of proposed algorithm, these parameters were optimized using a genetic algorithm.

A new transiction rule. The rule of the equation(7) is modified by:

$$J = \begin{cases} argmax_{u\ j_i^k}\{[\tau_{iu}(t)] \cdot [\eta_{iu}]\} & if\ q \leq q_0 \\ J & if\ q > q_0 \end{cases} \tag{12}$$

This rule allows the exploration. Where, an ant *k* is move through *i* and *j*, with a distribution *q* in a range *[0, 1]*, q_0 is a parameter adjusts in the range $(0 \leq q_0 \leq 0)$ y $J \in J_i^k$, is a state select based in

$$p_{ij}^k = \alpha \sin\beta \cdot \tau_{ij}^k(t) + \gamma \tag{13}$$

The transition rule, therefore is different (of equation 7) when $q \leq q_0$, this meaning is a heuristic knowledge characterized in the pheromone. The amount of pheromone $\tau_{ij} \in Z$, can be positive and negative, allowing a not-extinction, but rather to continue comparison between its these, is obtain the value more high of pheromone.

$$\Delta\tau_{ij}(t) = \frac{1}{L^+} where L^+ \in T^+ \tag{14}$$

The update rule allows a global update, only for the path best.

1. For all edge (i, j) initialize $\tau_{ij} = c$ and $\Delta\tau_{ij}(t) = 0$.
2. Put the *m*-ant's created with a frequency *f* in the node top.
3. Repeat
   a. Natural selection (GA Modified)
   b. For k:=1 to ms
      i. Select to *J* with a transition rule $p_{ij}^{k}(t)$
      ii. Move to ant to *J*
      iii. Update the tour with (6)
      iv. If *J* was visited (Kill ant)
      v. Else (*J* is part of the list)
   c. Calculate the L^k of the k-th ant.
   d. Update the short best path.
   e. For any edge (i, j) applied (13) and (14).
4. Until Find a path.
5. If find a path finish else go to step 2.

Figure 6. ACO Modified.

5. Experimental results

In this section, the accuracy of the proposed algorithms described above. Present different start node, implying different grade of complexity.

Firtstly obtain the graph of each environment, the same applied of the landmarks of init and finish, also the centroid of the initial node. Finally, applied the algorithms over each graph, search the shortest path.

6. Conclusions and perspectives

This work was implemented with call selection natural and evolution natural, through basict two types of ants: jobs and explorer. The offspring are considerated for the jobs, the best foragers and for the explorer, the offspring least have lost their path. Each ant have three gene, α, β and γ owned to transition function. The parameters was applied in the same algorithms, but, the best result is obtanained with the ACO-GA algorithm.

The implementation of the ACO-GA in a robot manipulator, is a job in prosess, but the first results prove the effectively of the same. See figures (9) and (10).

http://dx.doi.org/10.5772/54460

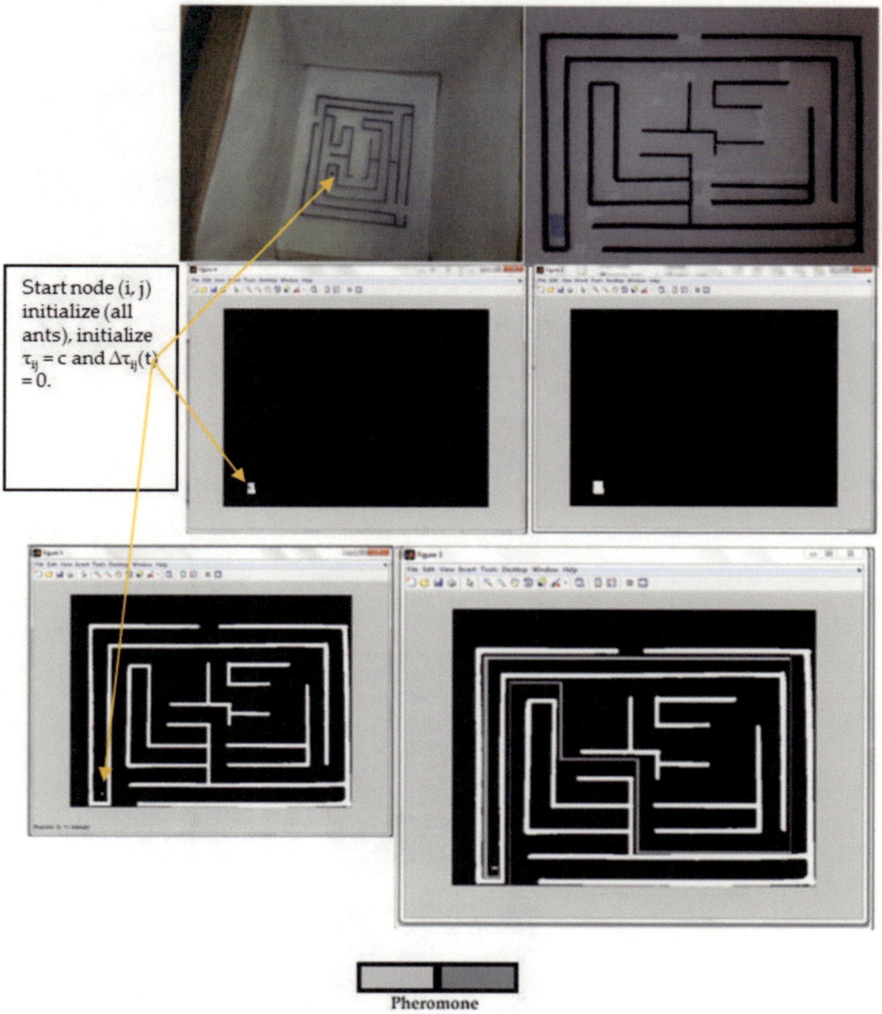

Figure 7. Images of Solution Process applied the ACO-GA Algorithm and parameters of table 1.

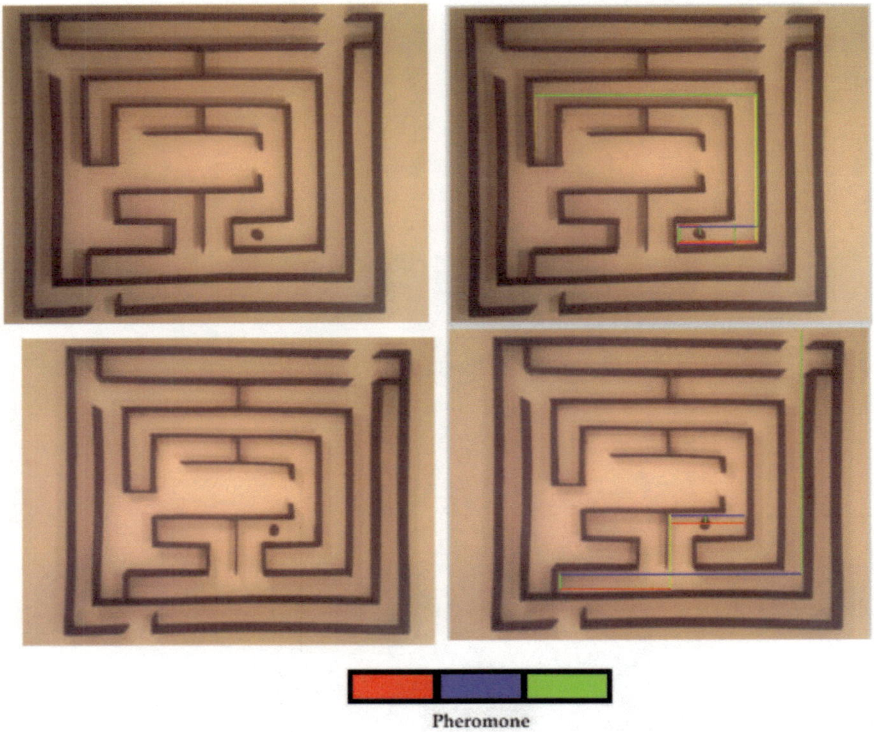

Figure 8. Images of Solution Process applied the ACO-GA Algorithm and parameters of table 1. Note that Different Start Node.

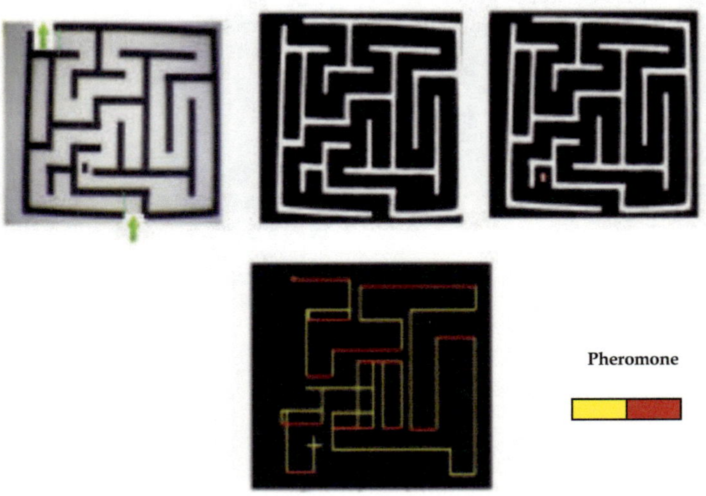

Figure 9. Solution to Labyrinth Applied ACO-algorithm.

http://dx.doi.org/10.5772/54460

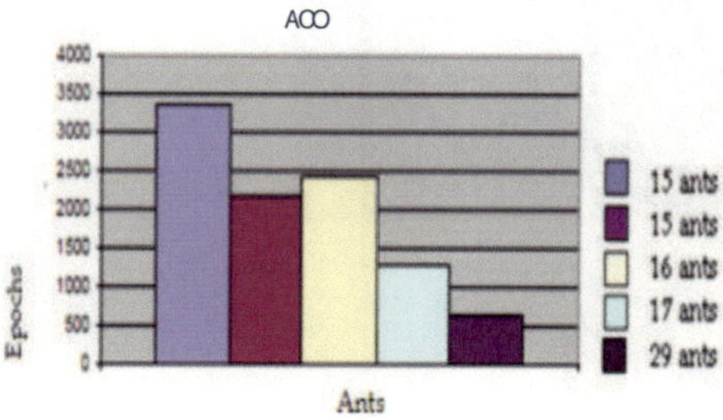

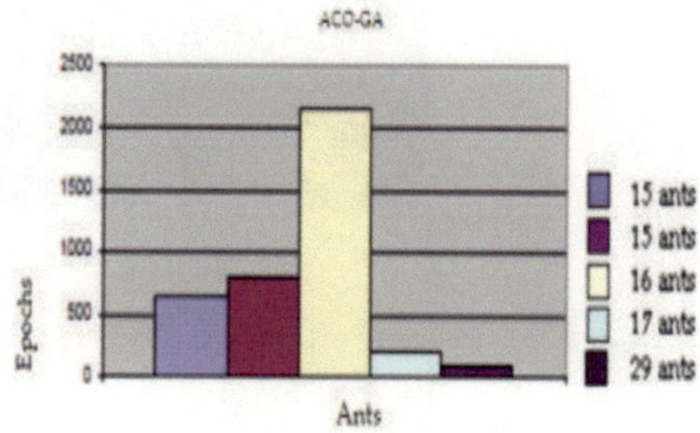

Figure 10. Example of a variation of epochs with (0 < α <1); β < γ or β > γ applied ACO and ACO-GA.

Value	Configuration 1	Configuration 2	Configuration 3	Configuration 4	Configuration 5
α	-4.86	-3.69	0.1	4.4	-1.8
β	1.1	-2.69	-3.3	2.6	1.34
γ	-1.7	0.7	-2.02	1.7	3.49
Ants	29	15	15	17	16
Epoch	105	643	794	196	2166
t_{mseg}	13	273	277	40	860

Figure 11. Best value applied to the best ACO and the best ACO-GA

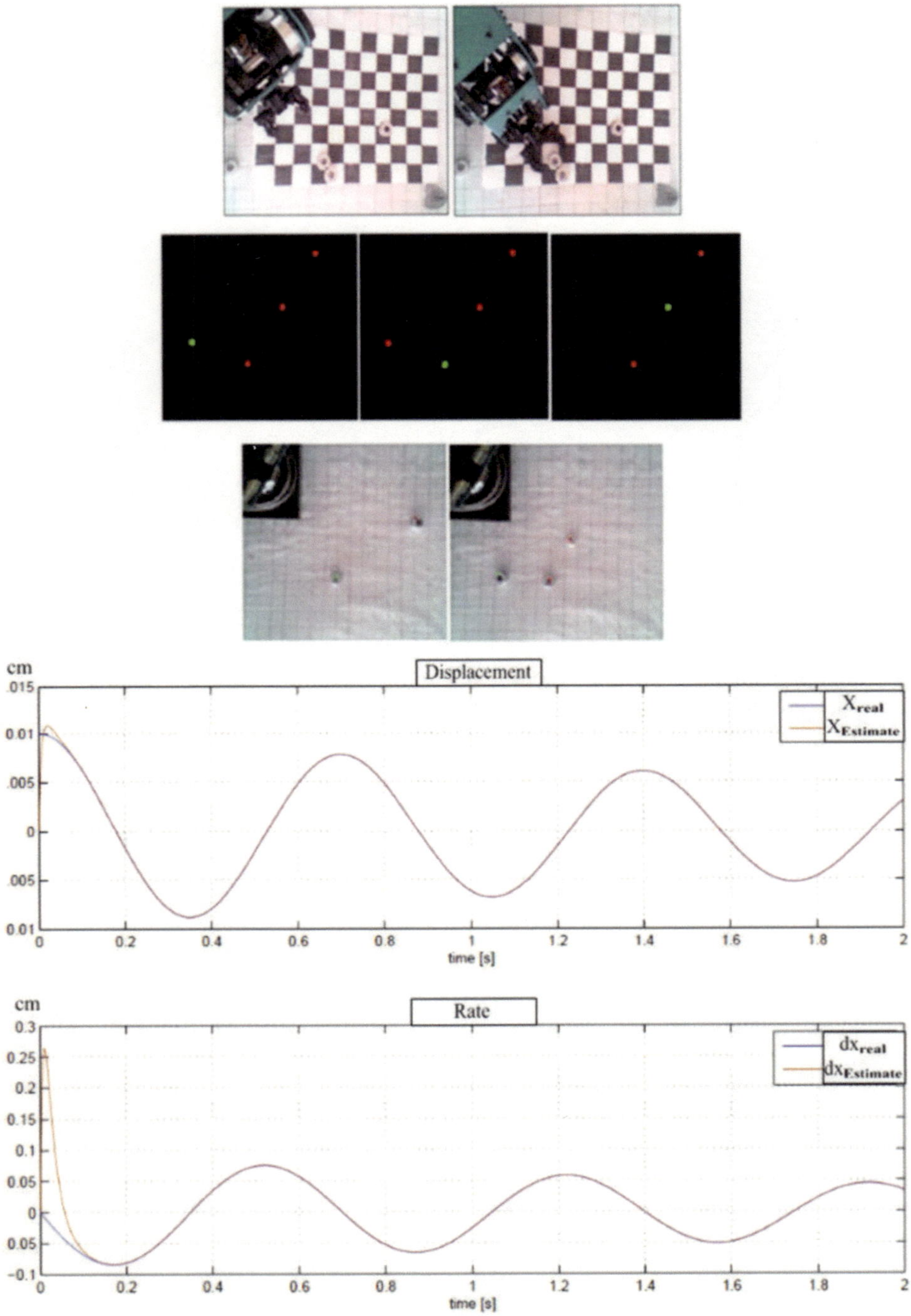

Figure 12. The robot manipulator select to piece of course to pheromone (green). Note, that the manipulator can't take the first piece. Graphics Displacement and Monitoring of the Manipulator respect to pheromone.

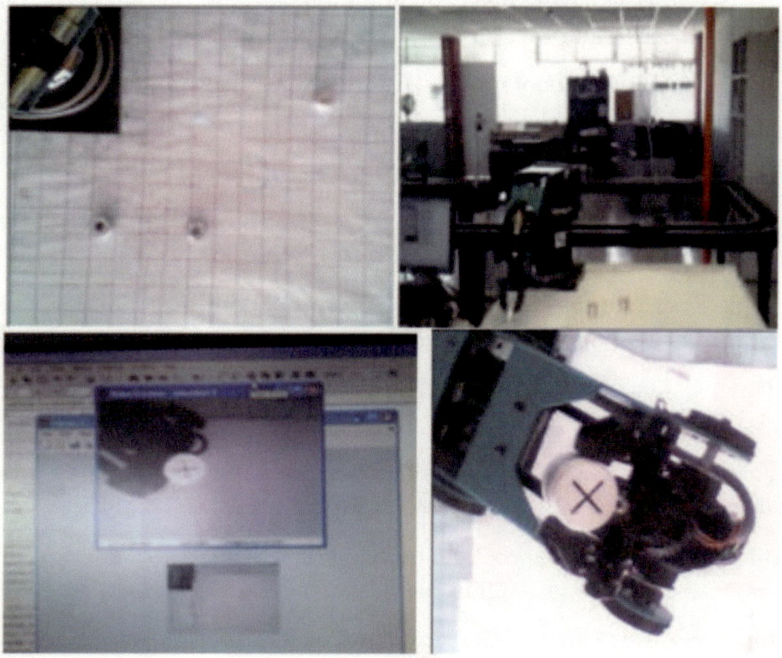

Figure 13. Besides using the ACO-Modified, is necessary calculate the distance of the first node through of de equation (6). Because the initial pose of manipulator can be "above" of the piece or well to distance not detectable by manipulator of the initial node, of manipulator makes it impossible of take.

Author details

Alejandra Cruz-Bernal*

Address all correspondence to: acruz@upgto.edu.mx

Polytechnic University of Guanajuato, Robotics Engineering Department, Community Juan Alonso, Cortázar, Guanajuato, Mexico

References

[1] Siegwart, R, & Nourbakhsh, I. R. (2004). Introduction to autonomous mobile robot. Massachusetts Institute of Technologypress, Cambridge, U.S.A.

[2] Borenstein, J, Everett, H. R, & Feng, L. Where am I? Sensors and Methods for Mobile Robot Positioning, Ann Arbor, University of Michigan,(1996). available at http://www-personal.engin.umich.edu/~johannb/position.htm), 184-186.

[3] Udupa, S. (1977). Collision detection and avoidance in computer controlled manipulator. PHD thesis, California Institute Technology, California, USA.

[4] Latombe, J. C. (1991). Robot motion planning. Kluwer Academic Publisher, Boston.

[5] Lozano-Perez T Wesley MA ((1979). An algorithm for planning collision-free paths among polyhedral obstacles. Commun ACM., , 22(10), 560-570.

[6] Li, L, Ye, T, Tan, M, & Chen, X. (2002). Present state and future development of mobile robot technology research. Robot., (24)5: 475-480.

[7] Siegwart, R, & Nourbakhsh, I. R. (2004). Introduction to autonomus mobile robot. Massachusets Institute of Technology Press, Cambridge, U.S.A.

[8] Dunlaing, C. O, & Yap, C. K. (1985). A retraction method for planning a motion of a disc. J. Algorithms, , 6, 104-111.

[9] Masehian, E, & Katebi, . (2007). Robot motion planning in dynamic environments with mobile obstacles and target. Int. J. Mech. Syst. Sci. Eng., 1(1): 20-25.

[10] Garrido, S, Moreno, L, Blanco, D, & Jurewicz, P. (2011). Path planning for mobile robot navigation using Voronoi diagram and fast marching. Int. J. Robot. Autom., , 2(1), 42-64.

[11] Lozano-perez, T. (1983). spatial planning: A configuration approach. IEEE T. Comput. C, , 32(3), 108-120.

[12] Zhu, D. J, & Latombe, J. C. (1989). New heuristic algorithms for efficient hierarchical path planning. Technical report STAN-CS-Computer Science Department, Stanford University, USA., 89-1279.

[13] Payton, D. W, Rosenblatt, J. K, & Keirsey, D. M. (1993). Grid-based for mobile robot. Robot Auton. Syst., , 11(1), 13-21.

[14] Likhachev, M, Ferguson, D, Gordon, G, Stentz, A, & Thrun, S. (2005). Anytime dynamic A*: An anytime, replanning algorithm. Proceedings of the international Conference on Automated Planning and Scheduling, , 262-271.

[15] Hachour, O. (2008). The processed genetic FPGA implementation for path planning of autonomous mobile robot. Int. J. Circ. Syst. Sig. Proc., , 2(2), 151-167.

[16] Hachour, O. (2008). Path planning of autonomous mobile robot. Int. J. Syst. Appl. Eng. Dev., , 4(2), 178-190.

[17] Zheng, T. G, Huan, H, & Aaron, S. (2007). Ant Colony System Algorithm for Real-Time Globally Optimal Path Planning of Mobile Robots. Acta. Automatica. Sinica, , 33(3), 279-285.

[18] Cheeseman, P, Smith, R, & Self, M. A stochastic map for uncertain spatial relationships. In 4th International Symposium on Robotic Research, MIT Press, (1987).

[19] Jhon Leonard and HFeder. Decoupled stochastic mapping for mobile robot and auto navigation. IEEE Journal Oceanic Engineering, 66, (2001). , 4(4), 561-571.

[20] Neira, J, & Tardos, J. D. Data association in stchocastic mapping using joint compatibility test. IEEE Transaction Robotics and Automation, (2001). , 890-897.

[21] Clark, S, Dissanayake, G, Newman, P, & Durrant-whyte, H. A Solution Localization and Map Building (SLAM) Problem. IEEE Journal of Robotics and Automation, June (2001). , 17(3)

[22] Michael Montemerlo SebastianFastslam: A factored solution totje simultaneous localization and mapping problem, http://citeseer.nj.nec.com/503340.html.

[23] Nebot, E. (2002). Simultaneous localization and mapping 2002 summer school. Australian centre field robotics. http://acfr.usyd.edu.au/homepages/academic/enebot/

[24] Duan, H. B, Zhang, X. Y, & Xu, C. F. Bio-Inspired Computing", Science Press, Beijing, ((2011).

[25] Pehlivanoglu, Y. V. A new vibrational genetic algorithm enhanced with a Voronoi diagram for path planning of autonomous UAV", Aerosp. Sci. Technol., (2012). , 16, 47-55.

[26] Ye, W, Ma, D. W, & Fan, H. D. Algorithm for low altitude penetration aircraft path planning with improved ant colony algorithm", Chinese J. Aeronaut., (2005). , 18, 304-309.

[27] Duan, H. B, Yu, Y. X, Zhang, X. Y, & Shao, S. Three-dimension path planning for UCAV using hybrid meta-heuristic ACO-DE algorithm", Simul. Model. Pract. Th., (2010). , 18, 1104-1115.

[28] Duan, H. B, Zhang, X. Y, Wu, J, & Ma, G. J. Max-min adaptive ant colony optimization approach to multi-UAVs coordinated trajectory replanning in dynamic and uncertain environments", J. Bionic. Eng., (2009). , 6, 161-173.

[29] Xu, C. F, Duan, H. B, & Liu, F. Chaotic artificial bee colony approach to uninhabited combat air vehicle (UCAV) path planning", Aerosp. Sci. Technol., (2010). , 14, 535-541.

[30] Duan, H. B, Liu, S. Q, & Wu, J. Novel intelligent water drops optimization approach to single UCAV smooth trajectory planning", Aerosp. Sci. Technol., (2009). , 13, 442-449.

[31] Canny, J, & Reif, J. (1987). New lower bound techniques for robot motion planning problems. Proceedings of IEEE Symposium on the Foundations of Computer Science, Los Angeles, California, , 49-60.

[32] Sugihara, K, & Smith, J. (1997). Genetic algorithms for adaptive motion planning of an autonomous mobile robot. Proceedings of the IEEE International Symposium on Computational Intelligence in Robotics and Automation, Monterey, California, , 138-143.

[33] Goss, S, Aron, S, Deneubourg, J. L, & Pasteels, J. M. (1989). Self-organized Shortcuts in the Argentine Ant. Naturwissenchaften pg. Springer-Verlag.(76), 579-581.

[34] Dorigo, M, Maniezzo, V, & Colorni, A. (1996). The Ant System: Optimization by a colony of cooperating agents", IEEE Transactions on Systems, Man and Cybernetics-Part-B, , 26(1), 1-13.

[35] Kennedy, J, & Eberhart, R. C. (1995). Particle Swarm Optimization. Proceedings of the IEEE International Conference on Neural Networks, Perth, Australia, , 1942-1948.

[36] Qin, Y. Q, Sun, D. B, Li, N, & Cen, Y. G. (2004). Path Planning for mobile robot using the particle swarm optimization with mutation operator. Proceedings of the IEEE International Conference on Machine Learning and Cybernetics, Shanghai, , 2473-2478.

[37] Zhang, Q. R, & Gu, G. C. (2008). Path planning based on improved binary particle swarm optimization algorithm. Proceedings of the IEEE International Conference on Robotics, Automation and Mechatronics, Chendu, China, , 462-466.

[38] Nasrollahy, A. Z. Javadi HHS ((2009). Using particle swarm optimization for robot path planning in dynamic environments with moving obstacles and target. Third European Symposium on computer modeling and simulation, Athens, Greece, , 60-65.

[39] Gong, D. W, Zhang, J. H, & Zhang, Y. (2011). Multi-objective particle swarm optimization for robot path planning in environment with danger sources. J. Comput., , 6(8), 1554-1561.

[40] Yang, X. S. (2011). Optimization Algorithms. Comput., optimization, methods and algorithms. SCI 356, , 13-31.

[41] Taylor, K. La Valle, M.S. "I-Bug: An Intensity-Based Bug Algorithm", Robotics and Automation, (2009). ICRA'09. IEEE International Conference, , 3981-3986.

[42] Parker, J. K, Khoogar, A. R, & Goldberg, D. E. Inverse kinematics ofredundant robots using genetic algorithms". Proc. IEEE ICRA, (1989). , 1, 271-276.

[43] Davidor, Y. Robot programming with a genetic algorithm" Proc. IEEEInt. Conf. on Computer Sys. & Soft. Eng. ((1990). , 186-191.

[44] Solano, J, & Jones, D. I. Generation of collision-free paths, a geneticapproach", IEEE Colloquium on Gen. Alg. for Control Sys. Eng. ((1993). , 5.

[45] Hocaoglu, C, & Sanderson, A. C. Planning multi-paths usingspeciation in genetic algorithms", Proc IEEE Int. Conf. on EvolutionaryComputation, ((1996). , 378-383.

[46] Gen, M, Runwei, C, & Dingwei, W. Genetic algorithms for solvingshortest path problems", Proc. IEEE Int. Conf. on Evolutionary Comput. ((1997). , 401-406.

[47] Kumar PratiharD.; Deb, K.; Ghosh, A. "Fuzzy-genetic algorithms and mobile robot navigation among static obstacles" In Proc. CEC'99, (1999). , 1

[48] Zein-sabatto, S, & Ramakrishnan, R. Multiple path planning for agroup of mobile robots in a 3D environment using genetic algorithms"Proc. IEEE Southeast, ((2002). , 359-363.

[49] Raja, P. And Pugazhenthi, S. "Optimal path planning of mobile robots: A review"International Journal of Physical Sciences (2012). , 7, 1314-1320.

[50] Wilson, L. A, Moore, M. D, Picarazzi, J. P, & Miquel, S. D. S. Parallel genetic algorithm for search and constrained multi-objectiveoptimization" Proc. Parallel and Distributed Processing Symp., ((2004). , 165.

[51] Qing, L, Xinhai, T, Sijiang, X, & Yingchun, Z. Optimum PathPlanning for Mobile Robots Based on a Hybrid Genetic Algorithm" InProc. HIS'06. ((2006). , 53-58.

[52] Qingfu, Z, Jianyong, S, Gaoxi, X, & Edward, T. EvolutionaryAlgorithms Refining a Heuristic: A Hybrid Method for Shared-PathProtections in WDM Networks Under SRLG Constraints", IEEE Trans.on Systems, Man and Cybernetics, Part B, (2007). , 37(1), 51-61.

[53] Masehian, E, & Sedighizadeh, D. Classic and Heuristic Approaches in Robot Motion Planning- A Chronogical Review", World Academy of Science, Engineering and Technology, ((2007). , 100-106.

[54] Dorigo, M. Optimization, learning and natural algorithms (in italian)," Ph.D. dissertation,Dipartimento di Elettronica, Politecnico di Milano, Italy, (1992).

[55] Deneubourg, J, Clip, L, Camazine, P. -L, & Ants, S. S. buses androbots-self-organization of transportation systems", Proc. FromPerception to Action, ((1994). , 12-23.

[56] Dorigo, M, & Gambardella, L. M. Ant Colony System: A CooperativeLearning Approach to the Traveling Salesman Problem," IEEE Trans. InEvolutionary Comput., (1997). , 1(1), 53-56.

[57] Xiaoping, F, Xiong, L, Sheng, Y, Shengyue, Y, & Heng, Z. Optimalpath planning for mobile robots based on intensified ant colonyoptimization algorithm" Proc. IEEE on Rob. Intel. Sys. & Sig.Processing, (2003). , 1, 131-136.

[58] Ying-tung, H, Cheng-long, C, & Cheng-chih, C. Ant colonyoptimization for best path planning" Proc. IEEE/ISCIT'04, , 2004, 109-113.

[59] Ramakrishnan, R, & Zein-sabatto, S. Multiple path planning for agroup of mobile robot in a 2-D environment using genetic algorithms" InProc. Of the IEEE Int. Conf. on SoutheastCon'01, ((2001). , 65-71.

[60] Mohamad, M. M, Dunnigan, M. W, & Taylor, N. K. Ant ColonyRobot Motion Planning" Proc. Int. Conf. on EUROCON'05. (2005). , 1, 213-216.

[61] Na Lv and Zuren FNumerical Potential Field and Ant ColonyOptimization Based Path Planning in Dynamic Environment", IEEEWCICA'06, (2006). , 2, 8966-8970.

[62] Raja, P, & Pugazhenthi, S. (2008). Path planning for a mobile robot to avoid polyhedral and curved obstacles. Int. J. Assist. Robotics. Mechatronics, , 9(2), 31-41.

[63] Raja, P, & Pugazhenthi, S. (2009). Path planning for a mobile robot using real coded genetic algorithm. Int. J. Assist. Robot. Syst., , 10(1), 27-39.

[64] Raja, P, & Pugazhenthi, S. (2009). Path planning for mobile robots in dynamic environments using particle swarm optimization. IEEE International Conference on Advances in Recent Technologies in Communication and Computing (ARTCom 2009), Kottayam, India, , 401-405.

[65] Raja, P, & Pugazhenthi, S. (2011). Path Planning for a mobile robot in dynamic environments. Int. J. Phys. Sci., , 6(20), 4721-4731.

[66] XiongCh, Yingying K, Xian F, and Quidi W; "A fas two-stage ACO algorithm for robotic planning" Neural Comp., and App., Springer-Verlag ((2011). DOI:s00521-011-0682-7.

[67] Carriker, W. F, Khosla, P. K, & Krogh, B. H. The use of simulated annealing to solve the mobile manipulator path planning problem", Proc. IEEE ICRA ((1990). , 204-209.

[68] Janabi-sharifi, F, & Vinke, D. Integration of the artificial potential field approach with simulated annealing for robot path planning" Proc. IEEE Int. Conf. on Intel. Control ((1993). , 536-541.

[69] Blackowiak, A. D, & Rajan, S. D. Multi-path arrival estimates using simulated annealing: application to crosshole tomography experiment", IEEE J. Oceanic Eng. (1995). , 20(3), 157-165.

[70] Park, M. G, & Lee, M. C. Experimental evaluation of robot path planning by artificial potential field approach with simulated annealing", Proc. SICE ((2002). , 4, 2190-2195.

[71] Miao, H. A multi-operator based simulated annealing approach for robot navigation in uncertain environments. ((2010). Int. J. Comput. Sci. Secur., , 4(1), 50-61.

[72] Qidan, Z, Yongjie, Y, & Zhuoyi, X. Robot Path Planning Based on Artificial Potential Field Approach with Simulated Annealing" Proc. ISDA'06, ((2006). , 622-627.

[73] Rencken, W. D. (1993). Concurrent Localization and Map Building for Mobile Robots Using Ultrasonic Sensors." Proceedings of the 1993 IEEE/RSJ International Conference on Intelligent Robotics and Systems, Yokohama, Japan, July 26-30, , 2192-2197.

[74] Edlinger, T, & Puttkamer, E. (1994). Exploration of an Indoor Environment by an Autonomous Mobile Robot." International Conference on Intelligent Robots and Systems (IROS'94). Munich, Germany, Sept. 12-16, , 1278-1284.

[75] Pehlivanoglu, Y. V. A new vibrational genetic algorithm enhanced with a Voronoi diagram for path planning of autonomous UAV", Aerosp. Sci. Technol., (2012). , 16, 47-55.

[76] Mata, M, Armingol, J. M, & Rodríguez, F. J. (2004). A deformable Model-Based Visual System for Mobile Robot Topologic Navigation" CICYT Project TAP , 99-0214.

[77] Dudek, G, & Jenkin, M. (2000). Computational Principles of Mobile Robotics, Cambridge University Press, Cambridge, UK

[78] Dorigo, M. and G. Di Caro, "The Ant Colony Optimization meta-heuristic," in New Ideas in Optimization, D. Corne et al., Eds., McGraw Hill, London, UK, (1999). , 11-32.

[79] Dorigo, M, & Di, G. Caro, and L.M. Gambardella, "Ant algorithms for discrete optimization," Artificial Life, (1999). , 5(2), 137-172.

[80] Deneubourg, J. -L, Aron, S, Goss, S, & Pasteels, J. -M. The self-organizing exploratory pattern of the argentine ant. Journal of Insect Behaviour, (1990). , 3, 159-168.

[81] Weise, T. Global Optimization Algorithms-Theory and Application"- Second edition e-book. ((2007).

[82] David, E. Goldberg. Genetic Algorithms in Search, Optimization, and Machine Learning.Addison-Wesley Longman Publishing Co., Inc. Boston, MA, USA, January (1989). 0-20115-767-5

[83] John Henry HollandAdaptation in Natural and Artificial Systems: An IntroductoryA-nalysis with Applications to Biology, Control, and Artificial Intelligence. The University of Michigan Press, Ann Arbor, 1975. 047-2-08460-797-8Reprinted by MIT Press, April(1992). NetLibrary, Inc.

[84] J°orgHeitk°otter and David Beasley, editors. Hitch-Hiker's Guide to Evolutionary-Computation: A List of Frequently Asked Questions (FAQ). ENCORE (The EvolutioN-ary Computation REpository Network), 1998. USENET: comp.ai.genetic. Onlineavailable at http://www.cse.dmu.ac.uk/~rij/gafaq/top.htm and http://alife.santafe.edu/~joke/encore/www/

[85] Hui-Chin TangCombined random number generator via the generalized Chinese remainder theorem. Journal of Computational and Applied Mathematics, May 15, (2002). 0377-0427doi:10.1016/S0377-0427(01)00424-1.Onlineavailable at http://dx.doi.org/10.1016/S0377-0427(01)00424-1, 142(2), 377-388.

[86] Blum, C, & Li, X. Swarm Intelligence: Swarm Intelligence in Optimization",Natural Computing Series, (2008). Part I, DOI:, 43-85.

[87] David, E. Goldberg. Genetic Algorithms in Search, Optimization, and Machine Learning.Addison-Wesley Longman Publishing Co., Inc. Boston, MA, USA, January (1989). 0-20115-767-5

[88] John Henry HollandGenetic Algorithms. Scientific American, July(1992). Online available at http://www.econ.iastate.edu/tesfatsi/holland.GAIntro.htmandhttp://www.cc.gatech.edu/~turk/bio_sim/articles/genetic_algorithm.pdf., 267(1), 44-50.

Chapter 4

A Comparative Study on Meta Heuristic Algorithms for Solving Multilevel Lot-Sizing Problems

Ikou Kaku, Yiyong Xiao and Yi Han

Additional information is available at the end of the chapter

http://dx.doi.org/10.5772/55279

1. Introduction

Material requirements planning (MRP) is an old field but still now plays an important role in coordinating replenishment decision for materials/components of complex product structure. As the key part of MRP system, the multilevel lot-sizing (MLLS) problem concerns how to determine the lot sizes for producing/procuring multiple items at different levels with quantitative interdependences, so as to minimize the total costs of production/procurement setup and inventory holding in the planning horizon. The problem is of great practical importance for the efficient operation of modern manufacturing and assembly processes and has been widely studied both in practice and in academic research over past half century. Optimal solution algorithms exist for the problem; however, only small instances can be solved in reasonable computational time because the problem is NP-hard (Steinberg and Napier, 1980). Early dynamic programming formulations used a network representation of the problem with a series structure (Zhangwill, 1968,1969) or an assembly structure (Crowston and Wagner,1973). Other optimal approaches involve the branch and bound algorithms (Afentakis et al., 1984, Afentakis and Gavish, 1986) that used a converting approach to change the classical formulation of the general structure into a simple but expanded assembly structure. As the MLLS problem is so common in practice and plays a fundamental role in MRP system, many heuristic approaches have also been developed, consisting first of the sequential application of the single-level lot-sizing models to each component of the product structure (Yelle,1979, Veral and LaForge,1985), and later, of the application of the multilevel lot-sizing models. The multilevel models quantify item interdependencies and thus perform better than the single-level based models (Blackburn and Millen, 1985, Coleman and McKnew, 1991).

Recently, meta-heuristic algorithms have been proposed to solve the MLLS problem with a low computational load. Examples of hybrid genetic algorithms (Dellaert and Jeunet, 2000, Dellaert et al., 2000), simulated annealing (Tang, 2004, Raza and Akgunduz, 2008), particle swarm optimization (Han et al, 2009, 2012a, 2012b), and soft optimization approach based on segmentation (Kaku and Xu, 2006, Kaku et al, 2010), ant colony optimization system (Pitakaso et al., 2007, Almeda, 2010), variable neighborhood search based approaches (Xiao et al., 2011a, 2011b, 2012), have been developed to solve the MLLS problem of large-scale. Those meta-heuristic algorithms outperform relative simplicity in solving the MLLS problems, together with their cost efficiency, make them appealing tool to industrials, however they are unable to guarantee an optimal solution. Hence those meta-heuristic algorithms that offer a reasonable trade-off between optimality and computational feasibility are highly advisable. It is very reasonable to consider the appropriateness of the algorithm, especially is which algorithm most appropriate for solving the MLLS problems?

In this chapter, We first review the meta-heuristic algorithms for solving the MLLS problems, especially focus on the implemental techniques and their effectives in those meta-heuristic algorithms. For simplicity the MLLS problems are limited with time-varying cost structures and no restrictive assumption on the product structure. Even so the solutions of the MLLS problems are not simply convex but becoming very complex with multi minimums when the cost structure is time-varying and the product structure is becoming general. Comparing those implement methods used in different algorithms we can find some essential properties of searching better solution of the MLLS problems. Using the properties therefore, we can specify the characteristics of the algorithms and indicate a direction on which more efficient algorithm will be developed.

Second, by using these properties as an example, we present a succinct approach—iterated variable neighborhood descent (IVND), a variant of variable neighborhood search (VNS), to efficiently solve the MLLS problem. To examine the performance of the new algorithm, different kinds of product structures were considered including the component commonality and multiple end-products, and 176 benchmark problems under different scales(small, medium and large) were used to test against in our computational experiments. The performance of the IVND algorithm were compared with those of three well-known algorithms in literatures—the hybrid genetic algorithm by Dellaert and Jeunet (2000a), the MMAS algorithm by Pitakaso et al. (2007), and the parallel genetic algorithm by by Homberger (2008), since they all tackled the same benchmark problems. The results show that the IVND algorithm is very competitive since it can on average find better solutions in less computing time than other three.

The rest of this chapter is organized as follows. Section 2 describes the MLLS problem. Section 3 gives an overview of related meta-heuristic algorithms firstly, and several implemental techniques used in the algorithms are discussed. Then section 4 explains the initial method and six implemental techniques used in IVND algorithm, and the scheme of the proposed IVND algorithm. In section 5, computational experiments are carried out on three 176 benchmark problems to test the new algorithm of efficiency and effectiveness and compared with existing algorithms. Finally, in section 7, we symmary the chapter.

2. The MLLS problems

The MLLS problem is considered to be a discrete-time, multilevel production/inventory system with an assembly structure and one finished item. We assume that external demand for the finished item is known up to the planning horizon, backlog is not allowed for any items, and the lead time for all production items is zero. Suppose that there are M items and the planning horizon is divided into N periods. Our purpose is to find the lot sizes of all items so as to minimize the sum of setup and inventory-holding costs, while ensuring that external demands for the end item are met over the N-period planning horizon.

To formulate this problem as an integer optimization problem, we use the same notation of Dellaert and Jeunet (2000a), as follows:

i : Index of items, $i = 1, 2, \ldots, M$

t : Index of periods, $t = 1, 2, \ldots, N$

H_i: Unit inventory-holding cost for item i

S_i: Setup cost for item i

$I_{i,t}$: Inventory level of item i at the end of period t

$x_{i,t}$: Binary decision index addressed to capture the setup cost for item i

$D_{i,t}$: Requirements for item i in period t

$P_{i,t}$: Production quantity for item i in period t

$C_{i,j}$: Quantity of item i required to produce one unit of item j

$\Gamma(i)$: set of immediate successors of items i

M: A large number

The objective function is the sum of setup and inventory-holding costs for all items over the entire planning horizon, denoted by TC (total cost). Then

$$TC = \sum_{i=1}^{M}\sum_{t=1}^{N}(H_i \cdot I_{i,t} + S_i \cdot x_{i,t}). \tag{1}$$

The MLLS problem is to minimize TC under the following constraints:

$$I_{i,t} = I_{i,t-1} + P_{i,t} - D_{i,t}, \tag{2}$$

$$D_{i,t} = \sum_{j \in \Gamma_i} C_{i,j} \cdot P_{j,t+l_j} \qquad \forall i \mid \Gamma_i \neq \varphi, \tag{3}$$

$$P_{i,t} - M \cdot x_{i,t} \leq 0, \tag{4}$$

$$I_{i,t} \geq 0, \quad P_{i,t} \geq 0, \qquad x_{i,t} \in \{0,1\}, \qquad \forall i,t. \tag{5}$$

where Equation 2 expresses the flow conservation constraint for item i. Note that, if item i is an end item (characterized by $\Gamma(i)=\varphi$), its demand is exogenously given, whereas if it is a component (such that $\Gamma(i)\neq\varphi$), its demand is defined by the production of its successors (items belonging to $\Gamma(i)$ as stated by Equation 3). Equation 3 guarantees that the amount $P_{j,t}$ of item j available in period t results from the exact combination of its predecessors (items belonging to Γ_i in period t). Equation 4 guarantees that a setup cost is incurred when a production is produced. Equation 5 states that backlog is not allowed, production is either positive or zero, and that decision variables are 0, 1 variables.

Because $x_{i,t} \in \{0, 1\}$ is a binary decision variable for item i in period t, $X = \{x_{i,t}\}_{M\times N}$ represents the solution space of the MLLS problem. Searching for an optimal solution of the MLLS problem is equivalent to finding a binary matrix that produces a minimum sum of the setup and inventory-holding costs. Basically, there exists an optimal solution if

$$x_{i,t} \cdot I_{i,t-1} = 0 \tag{6}$$

Equation 6 indicates that any optimal lot must cover an integer number of periods of future demand. We set the first column of X to be 1 to ensure that the initial production is feasible because backlog is not allowed for any item and the lead times are zero. Since there is an inner corner property for assembly structure (see Tang (2004)), we need to have $x_{i,t} \geq x_{k,t}$ if item creates internal demand for item k. Thus we need a constraint in order to guarantee that the matrix is feasible.

3. Meta-heuristic algorithms used to solve MLLS problems

The meta-heuristic algorithms are widely used to refer to simple, hybrid and population-based stochastic local searching (Hoos and Thomas 2005). They transfer the principle of evolution through mutation, recombination and selection of the fittest, which leads to the development of solutions that are better adapted for survival in a given environment, to solving computationally hard problems. However, those algorithms often seem to lack the capability of sufficient search intensification, that is, the ability to reach high-quality candidate solutions efficiently when a good starting position is given. Hence, in many cases, the performance of the algorithms for combinatorial problems can be significantly improved by adding some implemental techniques that are used to guide an underlying problem-specific heuristic. In this chapter, our interesting is on the mechanisms of those implemental techniques used to solve a special combinatorial optimization problem, i.e. MLLS problem. Hence we first review several existing meta-heuristic algorithms for solving the MLLS problems.

3.1. Soft optimization approach

Soft optimization approach (SOA) for solving the MLLS problems is based on a general sampling approach (Kaku and Xu, 2006; Kaku et al, 2010). The main merit of soft optimization approach is that it does not require any structure information about the objective function, so it can be used to treat optimization problems with complicated structures. However, it was shown that random sampling (for example simple uniform sampling) method cannot produce a good solution. Several experiments had been derived to find the characteristics of an optimal solution, and as a result applying the solution structure information of the MLLS problem to the sampling method may produce a better result than that arising from the simple uniform sampling method. A heuristic algorithm to segment the solution space with percentage of number of 1s has been developed and the performance improvement of solving MLLS problem was confirmed. It should be pointed that the SOA based on segmentation still remains the essential property of random sampling but limited with the searching ranges, however the adopted new solution(s) does not remain any information of the old solution(s). Therefore the improvement of solution performance can only be achieved by increasing the numbers of samples or by narrowing the range of segment.

3.2. Genetic algorithm

Genetic algorithm (GA) has been developed firstly for solving the MLLS problems in (Dellaert and Jeunet, 2000a, Dellaert et al. 2000b, Han et al. 2012a, 2012b). In fact, it firstly created the way that solving MLLS problems by using meta-heuristic algorithms. Several important contributions were achieved. Firstly a very general GA approach was developed and improved by using several specific genetic operators and a roulette rule to gather those operators had been implemented to treat the two dimensional chromosomes. Secondly, comparison studies had been provided to show that better solution could be obtained than those existing heuristic algorithms, based on several benchmarks data collected from literature. Later such benchmarks provide a platform of developing meta-heuristic algorithms and evaluating their performance. Because the complexity of MLLS problem and the flexibility and implement ability of GA are matching each other so that GA seems powerful and effective for solving MLLS problem. However, even several operators as single bit mutation; cumulative mutation; inversion; period crossover and product crossover were combined in the GA algorithm but what operators were effective in better solution searching process was not presented clearly. It is the point that we try to define and solve in this chapter.

3.3. Simulated annealing

Simulated annealing (SA) has been also developed to solve the MLLS problem (Tang,2004; Raza and Akgunduz,2008). It starts from a random initial solution and changing neighbouring states of the incumbent solution by a cooling process, in which the new solution is accepted or rejected according to a possibility specified by the Metropolis algorithm. Also parameters used in the algorithm had been investigated by using the analysis of variance approach. It had been reported that the SA is appropriate for solving the MLLS problem however verified only in very small test problems. Based on our understanding for SA, different from other meta-heuristic algorithms like GA, SA is rather like a local successive search approach from an initial solution. Then almost information of the old solution can be remained which may lead a long time to search better solution if it is far from the original solution. Also several implement methods con be used to improve the effective of SA (see Hoos and Thomas 2005). It is a general point to improve the effective of SA through shortening the cooling time with some other local searching methods.

3.4. Particle swarm optimization

Particle swarm optimization (PSO) is also a meta-heuristic algorithm formally introduced (Han et al,2009, 2011). It is a suitable and effective tool for continuous optimization problems. Recently the standard particle swarm optimization algorithm is also converted into a discrete version through redefining all the mathematical operators to solve the MLLS problems (Han et al, 2009). It starts its search procedure with a particle swarm. Each particle in the swarm keeps track of its coordinates in the problem space, which are associated with the best solution (fitness) it has achieved so far. This value is called pBest. Another "best" value tracked by the global version of the particle swarm optimization is the overall best value, and its location, obtained so far by any particle in the population, which is called gBest. Gather those so-called optimal factors into current solutions then they will converge to a better solution. It has been reported that comparing experiments with GA proposed in (Dellaert and Jeunet, 2000a, Dellaert et al. 2000b) had been executed by using the same benchmarks and better performance were obtained. Consider the essential mechanism of PSO, it is clear that those optimal factors (pBest and gBest) follow the information of the particle passed and direct where the better solution being. However, it has not been explained clearly that whether those optimal factors remained the required information when the PSO is converted into a discrete form.

3.5. Ant colony optimization

A special ant colony optimization (ACO) combined with linear program has been developed recently for solving the MLLS problem (Pitakaso et al. 2007, Almeda 2010). The basic idea of ant colony optimization is that a population of agents (artificial ants) repeatedly constructs solutions to a given instance of a combinatorial optimization problem. Ant colony optimization had been used to select the principle production decisions, i.e. for which period production for an item should be schedules in the MLLS problems. It starts from the top items down to the raw materials according to the ordering given by the bill of materials. The ant's decision for production in a certain period is based on the pheromone information as well as on the heuristic information if there is an external (primary) or internal (secondary) demand. The pheromone information represents the impact of a certain production decision on the objective values of previously generated solutions, i.e. the pheromone value is high if a certain production decision has led to good solution in previous iterations. After the selection of the production decisions, a standard LP solver has been used to solve the remaining linear problem. After all ants of an iteration have constructed a solution, the pheromone information is updated by the iteration best as well as the global best solutions. This approach has been reported works well for small and medium-size MLLS problems. However for large instances the solution method leads to high-quality results, but cannot beat highly specialized algorithms.

http://dx.doi.org/10.5772/55279

3.6. Variable neighbourhood search

Variable neighborhood search (VNS) is also used to solve the MLLS problem (Xiao et al., 2011a, 2011b, 2012). The main reasoning of this searching strategy, in comparison to most local search heuristics of past where only one neighborhood is used, is based on the idea of a systematic change of predefined and ordered multi neighborhoods within a local search. By introducing a set of distance-leveled neighborhoods and correlated exploration order, the variable neighborhood search algorithm can perform a high efficient searching in nearby neighborhoods where better solutions are more likely to be found.

There may other different meta-heuristic algorithms have been proposed for solving the MLLS problems, but it can be considered that the algorithms updated above can cover almost fields of the meta-heuristic so that the knowledge obtained in this chapter may has high applicable values. All of the meta-heuristic algorithms used to solve the MLLS problems are generally constructed by the algorithm describe in Fig.1 as follows.

Repeat the following step (1), (2) and (3):
(1)Find an initial solution(s) by using the *init* function.
(2)Repeat (a) and (b) steps:
(a)Find a new solution randomly in solution space by using the *step* function;
(b)Decide whether the new solution should be accepted.
(3)Terminate the search process by using the *terminate* function and output the best solution found.

Figure 1. General algorithm for solving the MLLS problem

In Fig. 1, at the beginning of the search process, an initial solution(s) is generated by using the function *init*. A simple *init* method used to generate the initial solution may be the random sampling method, and often several heuristic concepts of MLLS problem are employed to initialize the solution because they can help obtaining better performance. Moreover, the *init* methods are usually classified into two categories in terms of single solution or multi solutions (usually called population). Function *step* shows the own originality of the algorithm by using different implement techniques. By comparing the total costs of old and new solutions, it accepts usually the solution with smaller one as next incumbent solution. Finally, function *terminate*, a user-defined function such as numbers of calculation, coverage rate and so on, is used to terminate the program.

All of the implement techniques used in *step* function, which are represented in all of the meta-heuristic algorithms for solving the MLLS problems, can be summarized as below.

1. Single- bit mutation

Just one position (i,t) has randomly selected to change its value (from 0 to 1 or the reverse)

2. Cumulative mutation

When a single-bit mutation is performed on a given item, it may trigger mutating the value(s) of its predecessors.

3. Inversion

One position (i,t) has been randomly selected, then compare its value to that of its neighbor in position ($i,t+1$). If the two values are different from each other(1 and 0, or 1 and 0), then exchanges the two values. Note the last period $t=N$ should not be selected for inversion operation.

4. Period crossover

A point t in period (1, N) is randomly selected for two parents to produce off-springs by horizontally exchanging half part of their solutions behind period t.

5. Product crossover

An item i is randomly selected for two parents to produce off-springs by vertically exchanging half part of their solutions below item i.

Table 1 summaries what implement techniques and *init* function have been used in the existing meta-heuristicalgorithms.FromTable1itcanbeobservedthatallofthealgorithmsusethesingle-bit mutation method in their *step* function, but their ways of making the mutations are different. Clearly, SOA creates new solution(s) without using any previous information so that it may is recognized a non-implemental approach. Reversely SA uses single-bit and cumulative mutation based on incumbent solution therefore it reserves almost all of the previous information. Moreover, a random uphill technique is used in SA to escape from local optima so that the global optimal solution may is obtained. However a very long computing time is needed to get it. On the other hand, PSO uses the single-bit mutation method to create the new candidate in *step* function but starting with multiple initial solutions. According to the concept of original PSO, some information of solutions obtained before may be added into the construction of new solutions in order to increase the probability of generating better solutions. However, it needs a proof of such excellent property is guaranteed in the implemental process but is not appeared in the algorithm proposed before. It may is a challenge work for developing a new PSO algorithm for solving the MLLS problem. Finally, because the techniques of inversion and crossover (which were usually used in other combinational optimization problem such as a Travelling Salesman Problem) only have been used in GA, it is not able to compare them with other algorithms.

	Single- bit mutation	Cumulative mutation	Inversion	Period crossover	Product crossover	initial solution
SOA	—	—	—	—	—	many
GA	o	o	o	o	o	multi
SA	o	o	—	—	—	single
PSO	o	o	—	—	—	multi
ACO	o	—	—	—	—	single
VNS	o	o	o	—	—	single

Table 1. The implement techniques used in various algorithms

Note the implement techniques can change the states of the incumbent solution(s) to improve the performance with respect to total cost function, so that which implement technique could do how many contributions to the solution improvement is very important for the computing efficiency of MLLS problems. Here our interesting is on those implement techniques used in the above algorithms, which had been reported appropriate in their calculation situations. We define several criteria for evaluating the performance and effective of the implemental techniques. We firstly define distance-based neighborhood structures of the incumbent solution. The neighborhoods of incumbent solution are sets of feasible solutions associated with different distance measurements from the incumbent solutions. The distance means the exchanged number of different points of two incumbent solutions.

Definition 1. *Distance from incumbent solution*: For a set of feasible solutions of a MLLS problem, i.e., $X=\{x_{i,t}\}$, a solution X' belongs to the kth-distance of incumbent solution x, i.e. $N_k(x)$, if and only if it satisfies, $x' \in N_k(x) \Leftrightarrow \rho(x, x')=k$, where k is a positive integer. Distance between any two elements in in X, e.g., x and x', is measured by

$$\rho(x,x')=\left|x\setminus x'\right|=\left|x'\setminus x\right| \qquad \forall x,x'\in X \tag{7}$$

Where $|\bullet\setminus\bullet|$ denotes the number of different points between two solutions, i.e., $|\bullet\setminus\bullet|=\sum_{i=1}^{M}\sum_{t=1}^{N}|x_{i,t}-x_{i,t}^{'}|$

For example of a MLLS problem with 3 items and 3 periods, and three feasible solutions: x, x' and x'', which are as following,

$$x=\begin{vmatrix}1&0&0\\1&0&0\\1&1&1\end{vmatrix},\quad x'=\begin{vmatrix}1&0&0\\1&0&1\\1&1&1\end{vmatrix},\quad x''=\begin{vmatrix}1&0&0\\1&0&1\\1&0&1\end{vmatrix}$$

According to **Definition 1** above, we can get their distances such that: $\rho(x, x')=1$, $\rho(x', x'')=1$, $\rho(x, x'')=2$.

Therefore, creating a solution with k^{th} distance, i.e. $N_k(x)$, to the incumbent solution can be realized by changing the values of k different points of incumbent solution. It can be considered that less changes, e.g. $N_1(x)$, can avoid too much damage to the maybe good properties of the incumbent solution, in which some points may be already in its optimal positions. While multiple changes, e.g. $N_k(x)$ (k>1), lead a new solution to be very different from the incumbent solution, so it may also destroy the goodness of the original solution. However on the other hand local optimization may be overcame by multiple changes. Hence, following hypothesis may be considered to evaluate the performance and effective of an implement technique. Secondly we define range measurements that means the changing points are how far from the incumbent solutions. Eventually, we can evaluate those implemental techniques used in the algorithms to solve the MLLS problems by measuring the distance and range when the solution has been changed.

Definition 2. *Changing Range of incumbent solution*: Any elements belong to the kth-distance of incumbent solution x, i.e. $N_k(x)$, have a range in which the changed items and periods of incumbent solution have been limited.

Therefore, if the changing result of an incumbent solution by an implement technique falls into a small range, it seems be a local search and hence may give little influence on the total cost function. Otherwise a change of incumbent solution within a large range may be a global search increasing the probability of worse solutions found and resulting lower searching efficiency. Comparing the considerations of constructing mutation in the algorithms above, we can find that only short distance (for cumulative mutation, it is a very special case of long distance) has been executed in GA, SA and PSO with different implement techniques. For example, all of the algorithms use mutation to change the solution but only GA uses the probability of obtaining a good solution to increase the share rate of the operators. While SA uses a probability of accepting a worse solution to create an uphill ability of escaping from the traps of local optima, and PSO uses other two factors (*pBest* and *gBest*) to point a direction in which the optimal solution maybe exist. SOA and ACO are using basic random sampling principle to select the decisions in all positions of item and period. The difference is that SOA does not remain any information of previous solutions so large numbers of solution should be initialed and long distance (about half of items*periods) always existed, whereas ACO uses a level by level approach to do single-bit mutation in a solution so goodness of previous solution may has been remained with long distance. Finally, VNS directly use distances to search good solution so that its distance is controllable.

Next, regarding the other three implement techniques, i.e., the inversion, the item crossover, and the period crossover, which are not used in other algorithms except GA, we can find that the inversion is just a special mutation that changes the solution with two points distance. However crossover(s) may change the original solutions with a longer distance so only partial goodness of previous solution has been remained. In GA algorithm, the implement techniques with long and short distance are combined together, therefore it should be considered more effective for solving the MLLS problem. However, we have to say that those implement techniques used in above algorithms (includes GA) seem not effective in finding good solution. Because even a good solution exists near by the original solution, here is no way to guarantee that it will be found by above algorithms since the candidate solution is randomly generated. It can be considered that not only distance but also range should be used in the *step* function to find a better solution. However, two problems here need to answer. Can distance and range evaluate the effective of implement techniques using in the MLLS problem? How do the implement techniques should be applied?

For proofing our consideration above, simulation experiments were executed by using the general algorithm for solving the MLLS problems shown in Fig.1. Initial solution(s) is produced with a randomized cumulative Wagner and Whitin (RCWW) algorithm. The *step* function uses a GA algorithm, because all kinds of the implemental techniques had been included in the algorithm. We can control what the implemental technique should be used then evaluate the efficiency of the techniques. However the *terminate* functions used in different problem instances are different. In the experiments we first show the relationship among

http://dx.doi.org/10.5772/55279

distance range and searching effective. Then we investigate the performance effective of various implemental techniques. For calculating the distance, set $k \leftarrow 1$, and repeated to find randomly a better solution from $N_k(x)$ and accept it until non better solution could be found (indicated by 100 continuous tries without improvement). And then, search better solutions from next distance ($k \leftarrow k+1$) until $k > k_{max}$. The calculation is repeated for 10 runs in different rages and the averages are used. In the *step* of GA, each of the five operators (single-bit mutation, cumulative mutation, inversion, period crossover and product crossover) are used with a fixed probability 20%, to produce new generation. Initial populations are generated and maintained with a population of 50 solutions. In each generation, new 50 solutions are randomly generated and added into the populations, then genetic operation with the five operators was performed and related total cost has been calculated. In the selection, top 50 solutions starting from lowest total cost are remained as seeds for the next generation and the rest solutions are removed from the populations. We use a stop rule of maximum 50 generations in *terminate* function. The successful results are counted in terms of distance and range (maximum deviation item/ period position among changed points). If there is only one point changed, then the range is zero. Finaly, simulation is excuted by using the same banch marks of Dellaert and Jeunet (2000a).

Remark 1: Distance, range and searching effective

Table 2 and 3 show an example of better solutions with different distances in different ranges. Better solution is defined as that the new solutions are better than the incumbent, so we count the number of better solutions and calculate the ratio of different distances. It can be observed from Table 2 that different distances lead to different number of better solutions found. Most of them (94.82%) are found in the nearest neighbourhood with one point distance and the ratio decreases as the distance increasing, which indicates a less probability of finding better solution among those whose distance are long from the incumbent. However, the incumbent solution did be improved by candidate solutions from longer distance. Even so the results with same tendency can be observed from Table 3 in which a limited range has been used. However very different meanings can be observed from Table 3. Firstly, limiting the search range can lead to a more efficiency for searching better solutions, which is represented by the fact that the total number of better solutions found is about 4% more than that of the non-limited search, and it also leads to obtain a solution with a better total cost (comparing with Table 2). Secondly, even the number of better solutions are almost same in distance 1 (changing just one position of the incumbent solution), but the number of better solutions in distance 2 was about three times of that of non-limited search. That is, longer time and less effect were performed in distance 1 if the range is not limited. This observation can lead a considerable result of implementing a faster searching in distance 1 and a faster changing between distances. That is the superiors of limited searching range.

Distance	Better solutions	Ratio
1	3333	94.82%
2	135	3.84%

Distance	Better solutions	Ratio
3	28	0.80%
4	14	0.40%
5	5	0.14%
Total cost=826.23	3515	100.00%

Table 2. A non limited search in distances in small MLLS problems (Parameters: k_{max}=5, $\Delta i = \pm 5$, $\Delta t = \pm 12$)

Distance	Better solutions	Ratio
1	3232	88.57%
2	332	9.10%
3	55	1.51%
4	25	0.69%
5	5	0.14%
Total cost=824.37	3649	100%

Table 3. A limited search in distances in small MLLS problems (Parameters: k_{max}=5, $\Delta i = \pm 1$, $\Delta t = \pm 3$)

That means even the implemental techniques used in algorithms such as SA, PSO, and VNS are seemly different, but the results from them may be totally similar. In addition, GA uses other implement techniques like crossover(s), so it may lead a longer distance and improve the searching performance basically. Moreover, distance and range have a very flexible controllability to produce candidate solutions. It gives a very important observation that a special range which includes some heuristic information (such as period heuristics is effective but level heuristic is not effective, and so on) can improve the performance of implemental technique, therefore they should be used as some new implemental methods into the meta-heuristic algorithms.

Remark 2: effective of various implement techniques

Here five implemental techniques, i.e., single-bit mutation, cumulative mutation, inversion, product crossover, and period crossover, were tested by using GA algorithm. These implement techniques are used in the *step* function of our GA algorithm. The RCWW algorithm is used as the initial method to produce a population of 50 solutions as the first generation. Then, each of the five implemental techniques is selected with equal probability, namely, 20%, to produce a new generation, and each generation keeps only a population of 50 solutions after the selections by total cost function. The algorithm stops after 50 generations have been evolved. A solution is said to be a better solution if its objective cost is better than those of its parent and is counted in terms of changing distance and changing range from its parent. Therefore, simulation experiment is able to show the relationships among distance, range and searching effectives (represented by the number of better solutions found) of each implemental techni-

http://dx.doi.org/10.5772/55279

que. We represent the relationships among distance, range and searching effectives in a three dimensional figure, in which the dimensions are the *distance*, the *range* and the *number of better solutions found*. Then the distribution in the figures can show how the criteria of distance and range segmenting the searching effectives.

Firstly, it can be considered that the single-bit mutation and the inversion are very similar since the candidate solutions are always in distance 1 and range ±0 by single-bit mutation and always in distance 2 and range ±1 by inversion, so the better solutions found are always in distance 1 and range ±0 for the former and distance 2 and range ±1 for the latter, which have been verified in Fig.2 and Fig.3. Comparing Fig.2 and Fig.3, we also can find that the searching effective of reversion is little better than that of single-bit mutation because more better solutions can be found by reversion.

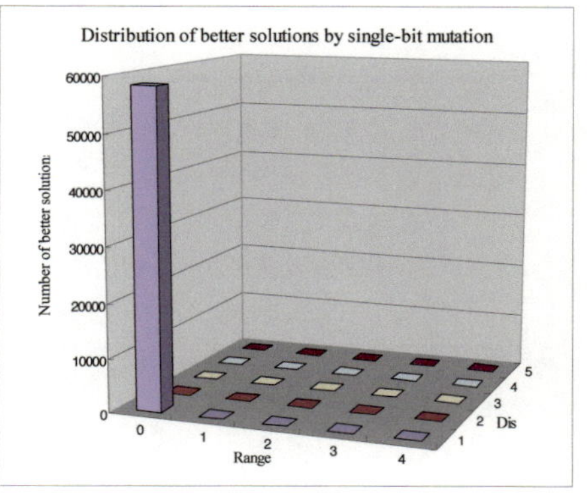

Figure 2. The result of single-bit mutation

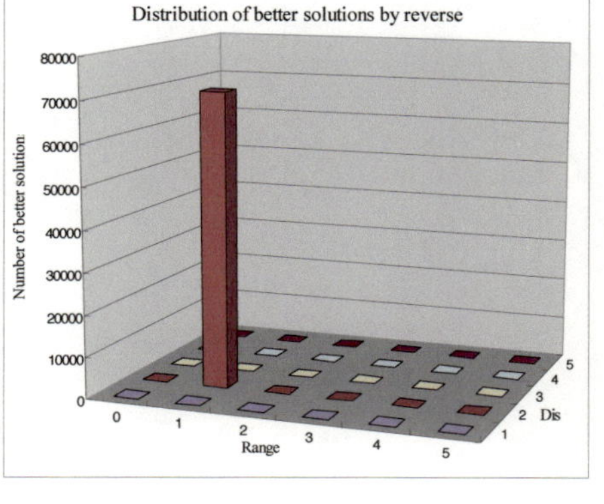

Figure 3. The result of reverse

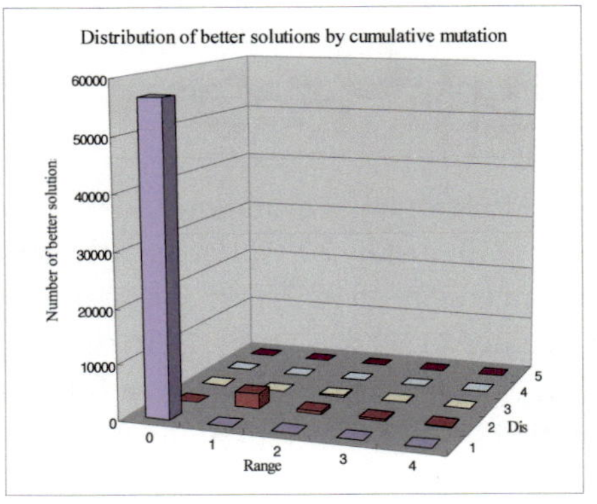

Figure 4. The result of cumulative mutation

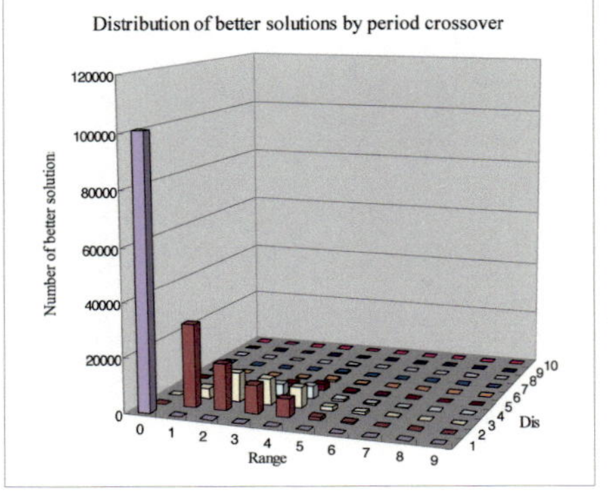

Figure 5. The result of period crossover

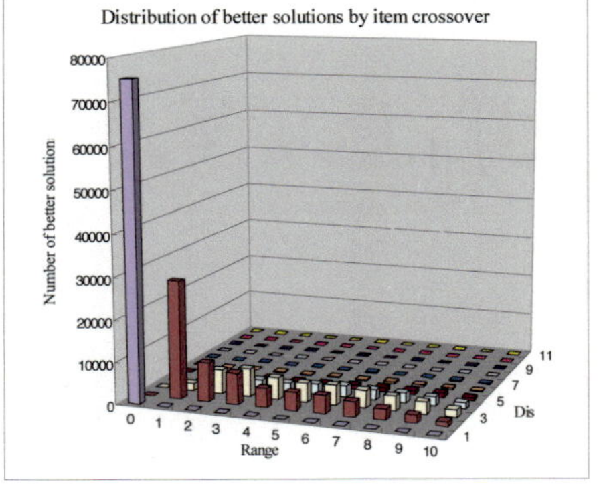

Figure 6. The result of item crossover

http://dx.doi.org/10.5772/55279

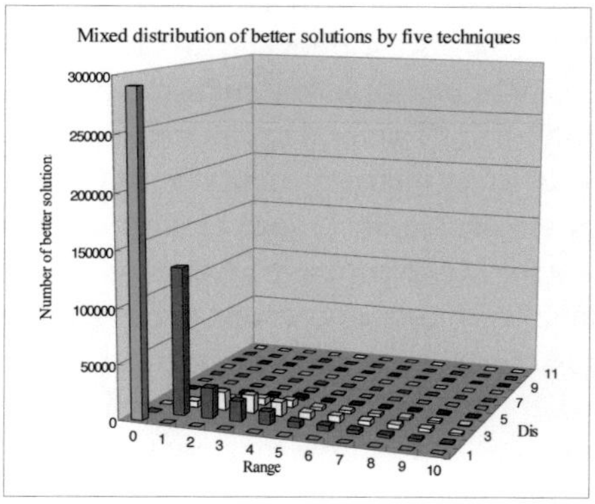

Figure 7. The mixed result of five implemental techniques

Secondly, it seems the cumulative mutation may trigger longer distance and larger range (than the single-bit mutation) to the incumbent solutions, the results of the experiment shown in Fig.4 can illustrate the correctness of this observation. Also it can be observed that only those with small distance and range are more effective in improving the performance of cost function.

Thirdly, the implemental techniques of item crossover and period crossover are more complex than cumulative mutation and reversion, and the offspring consequently may be associated with very large range and very long distance in comparison to their parents. Still, it can be observed from our experimental results in Fig.5 and Fig.6 that only those offspring with small distance and range are more effective on improving the fitness function. Moreover, comparing with simple implemental techniques (single-bit mutation, reversion and cummulative mutation), crossover techniques can achieve significent performance improvements in searching effective.

Finally in Fig.7, we show the mixed distribution of all the five implemental techniques. The results of simulation experiments show that a total signifecent effective of searching better solution can be obtained by using the mixed implemental techniques. Also repeatly, almost achievements of searching effective are in smaller distance and range. This phenominon may be used to conduct a more effective implemental technique in GA algorithms than pure free crossover.

However, for candidate solutions with larger range and longer distance, they still provided improvements on fitness function with probability so should not be ignored by any meta-heuristic algorithms for optimality purpose. Nevertherless, we can develop more effective and more efficient implemental techniques by matching to the ratio of better solution can be found in different ranges and distances. For example, those crossover operations resulting in offspring with too long distance are non-effective and should be avoided as possible.

4. An example: A IVNS algorithm for solving MLLS problems

The VNS/VND algorithm initiated by Mladenovic and Hansen (1997), Hansen and Mladenovic (2001) and Hansen et al. (2001, 2008), is a top-level methodology for solving the combinatorial optimization problems. Because its principle is simple and easily understood and implemented, it has been successfully applied to several optimization problems in different fields. The success of VNS is largely due to its enjoying many of the 11 desirable properties of meta-heuristic generalized by Hansen et al., (2008), such as simplicity, user-friendliness, efficiency, effectiveness, and so on. Since the MLLS problem is observed to share common characteristics, e.g., a binary decision variable, with those problems successfully solved by VNS/VND based algorithm, it is promising to develop an efficient algorithm for this problem (Xiao et al., 2011a, 2011b, 2012). Here an iterated variable neighborhood descent (IVND) algorithm, which is a variant of VNS, is proposed as an example to show the utility and performance improvement of considerations descripted above.

4.1. Initial method

We use a randomized cumulative Wagner and Whitin (RCWW) based approach to initialize the solution for our proposed IVNS algorithm. The RCWW method was introduced by Dellaert and Jeunet(2000a), of which the main idea is based on the fact that lot-sizing a product in the one period will trigger demands for its components in previous periods with leading time corrections(or in same period for the case of zero leading time). Therefore, the real setup cost of an item is in fact greater than its own setup cost and should be modified when using the wellknown sequentiail WW algorithm to generate a initial solution. The time-varying modified setup cost is a improved concept introduced by Dellaert et al(2000b, 2003) and used by Pitakaso et al(2007) which disposes of using a constant modified setup cost for the whole planning horizon; it suggested the costs might vary from one time period to the next, and reported good in getting better initial solutions.

In the IVND algorithm, we use the sequential WW algorithm based on randomly initialized constant modified setup cost to generate initial solutions. For each item i, its modified setup cost $S_i^{'}$ can be calculated recursively by

$$S_i^{'} = S_i + r\left[\sum_{j\in\Gamma_i^{-1}}\left(S_j + \frac{S_j^{'}}{\left|\Gamma_j^{-1}\right|}\right)\right] \tag{8}$$

where S_i is the original setup cost of item i, r is a random value uniformly distributed between [0,1], $\mid \Gamma_i^{-1} \mid$ is the set of immediate predecessors(components) of product i and $\mid \Gamma_i^{-1} \mid$ is its cardinality.

In addition to the modified setup cost, we also use the modified unit inventory holding cost to construct initial solutions. It is simply based on the consideration that a positive inventory balance of one product in one period causes not only its own inventory holding cost but also additional inventory holding cost from its predecessors because not all the demands for predecessors are met by timely production; some of them may also be satisfied by inventory. Therefore and similarly, the modified unit inventory holding cost of product i, i.e., $H_i^{'}$ can be calculated recursively by

$$H_i^{'} = H_i + q\left[\sum_{j\in\Gamma_i^{-1}}\left(H_j + \frac{H_j^{'}}{\left|\Gamma_j^{-1}\right|}\right)\right] \tag{9}$$

where H_i is the original unit inventory holding cost of product i and q is a random value uniformly distributed between [0,1].

4.2. Implemental techniques

Here six implemental techniques are used in the IVND algorithm which are integrated together to deliver good performance in the computing experiments.

1. *Limit the changing range of incumbent solution within one item*. Limit the changing range of incumbent solution within one item, i.e., $N_1(x)$, when exploring a neighborhood farther than $N_1(x)$. That is, when multiple mutations are done on incumbent solution, they must occur on same item but different periods.

2. *All mutations are limited between the first period and the last period that have positive demand.* This technique makes the search algorithm to avoid invalid mutations. Nevertheless, the first period with positive demand should be fixed with 1.

3. *No demand, no setup*. Mutation must not try of arranging setups for products in periods without positive demand, which is obviously non-optimal operation and should be banned in the whole searching process.

4. *Triggerrecursive mutations*. A mutation of canceling a setup for a product in a period will trigger recursive mutations on all of its ancestors. While a mutation of canceling a setup occurs, e.g. changing the value of bit x_{it} from 1 to 0, it withdraws demands for the immediate predecessors in previous periods of leading time. As a consequence, some of these predecessors their demands may drop to zero such that their setups (if they have) in these periods should be canceled at the same time; other predecessors who remain non-zero demands due to product commonality should remain unchanged. The recursive mutations are only triggered for cancellation of a setup for production; they will not occur when arranging a setup.

5. *Shift a setup rather than cancel a setup*. When the setup for product i at period t need to be canceled, try to shift the setup to the first period with positive demand behind t, rather than simply cancel it. For example, when x_{it} is to be canceled, find the first period t^* behind t of product i that satisfies $D_{it^*}>0$ and arrange a setup by setting $x_{it^*}\leftarrow 1$ if x_{it^*} is 0. Notably, this arrangement of this setup will also trigger recursive mutations.

6. *Only affected products and periods are recalculated of their inventory holding costs and setup costs.* Different to other evolutionary algorithms like GA and PSO where a group of incumbent solutions have to be maintained, the IVND algorithm has only one incumbent solution. In fact, when a mutation occurs, most area of the solution states including setup matrix Y_{it}, lot-sizing matrix X_{it} and demand matrix D_{it} are remain unchanged. Thus, it just needs to recalculate the affected products and the affected periods of the setup cost and inventory holding cost after a mutation operation. By taking this advantage, the computing efficiency of IVND algorithm can be significantly improved since the recalculation of the objective function--the most time-consuming part of IVND algorithm, are avoided.

The above six implemental techniques are all used in our proposed IVND algorithm to mutate the incumbent solution into its neighborhood. Steps of implementing these techniques on neighborhood search, e.g., neighborhood $N_k(x)$, can be explained by Fig.8.

To generate a candidate solution from neighborhood $N_k(x)$ of the incumbent solution x:

(1)Select randomly k bits of x, e.g., $x_{i,t_1}, x_{i,t_2}, ..., x_{i,t_k}$, and sequentially mutate them. The first three implement techniques mentioned above must follow in the selection: the first implemental technique that the to-be bits must be within an identical item; the second implemental technique that the to-be mutated periods should between the first period and last period with positive demand; the third implemental technique that those periods without demand should not be selected for mutation.

(2)For each mutation from 1 to 0(noticeably not including those from 0 to 1), the forth implemental technique must be followed to trigger recursive mutations toward its predecessors with zero demand. In the recursive mutation process, the fifth implemental technique must be implemented to try of shifting the setup to the first sequential period with positive demand, rather than simply removed it.

(3)Whenever a bit of the incumbent solution is changed, the sixth implemental technique is implemented to recalculate the objective function just by recalculating the affected items and their periods.

Figure 8. The implementation of implemental techniques

Although the new solutions from $N_k(x)$ may has a greater than k unit distance from the incumbent solution x after implemented with these six implemental techniques, it is still considered as a member of $N_k(x)$. These implemental techniques are only deemed as additional actions implemented on the new solution toward better solution. Moreover, benefiting from these actions, higher efficiency of VNS algorithm could be consequently anticipated, which has been confirmed in the experiments of Section 4.

4.3. The IVND algorithm

The algorithm IVND is a variant of the basic VND algorithm. It starts from initiating a solution as the incumbent solution, and then launches a VND search. The VND search repeatedly tries of finding a better solution in the nearby neighborhood of the incumbent solution and moves to the better solution found; if a better solution cannot be found in current neighborhood, then go to explore a father neighborhood until the farthest neighborhood is reached. Once the VND process is stopped(characterized by the farthest neighborhood been explored), another initial solution is randomly generated and restarts the VND search again. This simply iterated search

http://dx.doi.org/10.5772/55279

process loops until the stop condition is met. The stop condition can be a user-specified computing time or a maximum span between two restarts without improvement on the best solution found. In our experiments of the next section, we use the later one, i.e., a fixed times of continuous restarts without improvement, as the stop condition. The basic scheme the proposed IVND algorithm is illustrated in Fig. 9.

Define the set of neighborhood structures N_k, k=1,…,k_{max}, that will be used in the search; choose a stop condition.
Repeat the following step (1), (2) and (3) until the stop condition is met:
(1)Find an initial solution x_0 by using RCWW algorithm
(2)Set $k \leftarrow 1$, $n \leftarrow 0$;
(3)Until $k=k_{max}$ repeat (a), (b), and (c) steps:
  (a)Find at random a solution x' in $N_k(x)$;
  (b)Move or not: if x' is better than x, then $x \leftarrow x'$, $k \leftarrow 1$ and $n \leftarrow 0$, go to step (a) ; otherwise, $n \leftarrow n+1$;
  (c) If $n=N$, then shift to search a farther neighborhood by $k \leftarrow k+1$ and reset $n \leftarrow 0$;
(4)Output the best solution found.

Figure 9. The IVND algorithm for MLLS problem

There are three parameters, i.e., P, N, and K_{max}, in the IVND algorithm for determining the tradeoff between searching efficiency and the quality of final solution. The first parameter P is a positive number which serves as a stop condition indicating the maximum span between two restarts without improvement on best solution found. The second parameter N is the maximum number of explorations between two improvements within a neighborhood. If a better solution cannot be found after N times of explorations in the neighborhood $N_k(x)$, it is then deemed as explored and the algorithm goes to explore a farther neighborhood by $k \leftarrow k+1$. The third parameter K_{max} is the traditional parameter for VND search indicating the farthest neighborhood that the algorithm will go.

5. Computational experiments and the results

5.1. Problem instances

Three sets of MLLS problem instances under different scales(small, medium and large) are used to test the performance of the proposed IVND algorithm. The first set consists of 96 small-sized MLLS problems involving 5-item assembly structure over a 12-period planning horizon, which was developed by Coleman and McKnew (1991) on the basis of work by Veral and LaForge (1985) and Benton and Srivastava (1985), and also used by Dellaert and Jeunet (2000a). In the 96 small-sized problems, four typical product structures with an one-to-one production ratio are considered, and the lead times of all items are zero. For each product structure, four cost combinations are considered, which assign each individual item with different setup costs and different unit holding costs. Six independent demand patterns with variations to reflect low, medium and high demand are considered over a 12-period planning horizon. Therefore, these combinations produce $4 \times 4 \times 6 = 96$ problems for testing. The optimal solutions of 96 benchmark problem are previously known so that can serve as benchmark for testing against the optimality of the new algorithm.

The second set consists of 40 medium-sized MLLS problems involving 40/50-item product structure over a 12/24-period planning horizon, which are based on the product structures published by Afentakis et al. (1984), Afentakis and Gavish (1986), and Dellaert and Jeunet (2000). In the 40 medium-sized problems, four product structures with an one-to-one production ratio are constructed. Two of them are 50-item assembly structures with 5 and 9 levels, respectively. The other two are 40-item general structure with 8 and 6 levels, respectively. All lead times were set to zero. Two planning horizons were used: 12 and 24 periods. For each product structure and planning horizon, five test problems were generated, such that a total number of $4 \times 2 \times 5 = 40$ problems could be used for testing.

The third set covers the 40 problem instances with a problem size of 500 products and 36/52 periods synthesized by Dellaert and Jeunet (2000). There are 20 different product structures with one-to-one production ratio and different commonality indices[1]. The first 5 instances are pure assembly structures with one end-product. The instances from 6 to 20 are all general structure with five end-products and different communality indices ranges from 1.5 to 2.4. The first 20 instances are all over a 36-period planning horizon; the second 20 instances are of the same product structures of the first 20 instances but over a 52-period planning horizon. The demands are different for each instances and only on end-products.

Since the hybrid GA algorithm developed by Dellaert and Jeunet (2000a) is the first meta-heuristic algorithm for solving the MLLS problem, it was always selected as a benchmark algorithm for comparison with newly proposed algorithm. Therefore, we compared the performance of our IVND algorithm with the hybrid GA algorithm on the all instances of three different scales. We also compared our IVND algorithm with the MMAS algorithm developed by Pitakaso et al.(2007), and the parallel GA algorithm developed by Homberger (2008) since both of them used the same three set of instances used in this paper.

5.2. Test environment

The IVND algorithm under examination were coded in VC++6.0 and ran on a notebook computer equipped with a 1.6G CPU operating under Windows XP system. We fixed the parameter K_{max} to be 5 for all experiments, and let the parameter P and N changeable to fit for the different size of problem. The symbol 'IVND$_N^P$' specifies the IVND algorithm with the parameter P and N, e.g., IVND$_{200}^{50}$ indicates P=50, N=200, and K_{max}=5 by default. The effect of individual parameter on the quality of solution was tested in section 5.6.

5.3. Small-sized MLLS problems

We repeatedly ran IVND$_{200}^{50}$ on the 96 small-sized MLLS problems for 10 times and got 960 results among which 956 were the optimal results so the optimality was 99.58% indicated by

1 Commonality index is the average number of successors of all items in a product structure

the column *Best solutions found(%)*. The column *average time(s)* indicates the average computing time in second of one run for each problem. The average result of 10 and the minimum result of 10 are both shown in Table 4 and compared to the HGA algorithm of Dellaert and Jeunet (2000a), the MMAS algorithm of Pitakaso et al.(2007) and the PGA algorithm of Homberger (2008). It can be observed from Table 4 that $IVND^{50}_{200}$ uses 0.7 second to find 100% optimal solutions of 96 benchmark problems. Although the PGAC and the GA3000 can also find 100% optimal solutions, they take longer computing time and also take the advantage of hardware (for PGAC 30 processors were used to make a parallel calculation). After that, we adjust the parameter P from 50 to 200 and repeatedly ran $IVND^{200}_{200}$ on the 96 problems for 10 times again. Surprisingly, we got 960 optimal solutions (100% optimality) with computing time of 0.27 second.

Method	Avg. cost	Best solutions found (%)	Mean dev. if best solution not found	Average time(s)	CPU type	Number of processors	Sources
HGA_{50}	810.74	96..88	0.26	5.14s	--	1	Dellaert et al.(2000)
MMAS	810.79	92.71	0.26	<1s	P4 1.5G	1	Pitakaso et al.(2007)
GA_{100}	811.98	75.00	0.68	5s	P4 2.4G	1	Homberger(2008)
GA_{3000}	**810.67**	**100.00**	**0.00**	**5s**	**P4 2.4G**	**1**	**Homberger(2008)**
PGAI	810.81	94.79	0.28	5s	P4 2.4G	30	Homberger(2008)
PGAC	**810.67**	**100.00**	**0.00**	**5s**	**P4 2.4G**	**30**	**Homberger(2008)**
$IVND^{50}_{100}$ (Avg. of 10)	810.69	99.58	0.02	0.07s	NB 1.6G	1	IVND
$IVND^{50}_{100}$ (Min. Of 10)	**810.67**	**100.00**	**0.00**	**0.7s**	**NB 1.6G**	**1**	**IVND**
$IVND^{200}_{200}$(Avg. Of 10)	**810.67**	**100.00**	**0.00**	**0.27s**	**NB 1.6G**	**1**	**IVND**
OPT.	**810.67**	**100.00**	**0.00**	**--**	**--**	**-**	**--**

Table 4. Comparing IVND with existing algorithms on 96 small-sized problems

5.4. Medium-sized MLLS problems

Secondly, we ran $IVND^{100}_{600}$ algorithm on 40 medium-sized MLLS benchmark problems and repeated 10 runs. We summarize the 400 results and compare them with the existing algorithms in Table 5. More detailed results of 40 problems are listed in Table 6 where the previous best known solutions summarized by Homberger(2008) are also listed for comparison. After that, we repeatedly ran $IVND^{100}_{600}$ algorithm for several times and updated the best solutions for these 40 medium-sized problems which are listed in column *new best solution* in Table 6.

Method	Avg. cost	Optimality on previous best solutions (%)	Comp. Time(s)	CPU type	Number of processors	Sources
HGA_{250*}	263,931.8	17.50	<60s	--	1	Dellaert et all(2000)
MMAS	263,796.3	22.50	<20s	P4 1.5G	1	Pitakaso et al.(2007)
GA_{100}	271,268.2	0.00	60s	P4 2.4G	1	Homberger(2008)
GA_{3000}	266,019.8	15.00	60s	P4 2.4G	1	Homberger(2008)
PGAI	267,881.4	0.00	60s	P4 2.4G	30	Homberger(2008)
PGAC	263,359.6	65.00	60s	P4 2.4G	30	Homberger(2008)
$IVND_{600}^{100}$(Avg. of 10)	263,528.5	30.00	2.67	NB 1.6G	1	IVND
$IVND_{600}^{100}$ (Min. of 10)	263,398.8	60.00	26.7	NB 1.6G	1	IVND
Prev. best solution	263,199.8	--	--	--	--	--
New best solution	260,678.3	--	--	--	-	--

Table 5. Comparing IVND with existing algorithms on 40 medium-sized problems

It can be observed from Table 5 that the PGAC and $IVND_{600}^{100}$ (Min. of 10) algorithm are among the best and very close to each other. Although the optimality of PGAC (65%) is better than that of $IVND_{600}^{100}$ (Min. of 10) (60%) in terms of the baseline of previous best known solutions, it may drop at least 17% if in terms of new best solutions since 12 of 40 problems had been updated their best known solutions by IVND algorithm(see the column *new best solution* in Table 6) and 7 of the 12 updated problems' previous best known solution were previously obtained by PGAC. Furthermore, by taking account into consideration of hardware advantage of the PGAC algorithm(multiple processors and higher CPU speed), we can say that the IVND algorithm performances at least as best as the PGAC algorithm on medium-sized problems, if not better than.

	Instance				$IVND_{400}$		Prev. best Solution	New best solution	New method
	S	D	I	P	Avg. of 10	Min. of 10			
0	1	1	50	12	196,084	196,084	**194,571**	**194,571**	B&B
1	1	2	50	12	165,682	165,632	**165,110**	**165,110**	B&B
2	1	3	50	12	**201,226**	**201,226**	**201,226**	**201,226**	B&B
3	1	4	50	12	188,010	188,010	**187,790**	**187,790**	B&B
4	1	5	50	12	161,561	161,561	**161,304**	**161,304**	B&B
5	2	1	50	12	**179,761**	**179,761**	**179,762**	**179,761**	B&B

	Instance				IVND$_{400}$		Prev. best	New best	New
	S	D	I	P	Avg. of 10	Min. of 10	Solution	solution	method
6	2	2	50	12	**155,938**	**155,938**	**155,938**	**155,938**	B&B
7	2	3	50	12	**183,219**	**183,219**	**183,219**	**183,219**	B&B
8	2	4	50	12	136,474	**136,462**	**136,462**	**136,462**	B&B
9	2	5	50	12	186,645	**186,597**	**186,597**	**186,597**	B&B
10	3	1	40	12	**148,004**	**148,004**	**148,004**	**148,004**	PGAC
11	3	2	40	12	197,727	**197,695**	**197,695**	**197,695**	PGAC
12	3	3	40	12	**160,693**	**160,693**	**160,693**	**160,693**	MMAS
13	3	4	40	12	**184,358**	**184,358**	**184,358**	**184,358**	PGAC
14	3	5	40	12	**161,457**	**161,457**	**161,457**	**161,457**	PGAC
15	4	1	40	12	185,507	**185,170**	**185,170**	**185,161**	PGAC→IVND
16	4	2	40	12	**185,542**	**185,542**	**185,542**	**185,542**	PGAC
17	4	3	40	12	192,794	192,794	**192,157**	**192,157**	MMAS
18	4	4	40	12	136,884	**136,757**	**136,764**	**136,757**	PGAC→IVND
19	4	5	40	12	166,180	166,122	**166,041**	**166,041**	PGAC
20	1	6	50	24	344,173	343,855	**343,207**	**343,207**	PGAC
21	1	7	50	24	293,692	293,373	**292,908**	**292,908**	HGA
22	1	8	50	24	356,224	355,823	**355,111**	**355,111**	HGA
23	1	9	50	24	325,701	**325,278**	**325,304**	**325,278**	PGAC
24	1	10	50	24	386,322	**386,059**	**386,082**	**385,954**	HGA→IVND
25	2	6	50	24	341,087	341,033	**340,686**	**340,686**	HGA
26	2	7	50	24	378,876	**378,845**	**378,845**	**378,845**	HGA
27	2	8	50	24	346,615	346,371	**346,563**	**346,358**	HGA→IVND
28	2	9	50	24	413,120	412,511	**411,997**	**411,997**	HGA
29	2	10	50	24	390,385	**390,233**	**390,410**	**390,233**	PGCA→IVND
30	3	6	40	24	**344,970**	**344,970**	**344,970**	**344,970**	HGA
31	3	7	40	24	352,641	**352,634**	**352,634**	**352,634**	PGAC
32	3	8	40	24	356,626	356,456	**356,427**	**356,323**	PGAC→IVND
33	3	9	40	24	411,565	**411,438**	**411,509**	**411,438**	MMAS→IVND
34	3	10	40	24	**401,732**	**401,732**	**401,732**	**401,732**	HGA
35	4	6	40	24	289,935	**289,846**	**289,883**	**289,846**	PGAC→IVND
36	4	7	40	24	339,548	339,299	**337,913**	**337,913**	MMAS
37	4	8	40	24	320,920	320,426	**319,905**	**319,905**	PGCA

	Instance				$IVND_{400}$		Prev. best	New best	New
	S	D	I	P	Avg. of 10	Min. of 10	Solution	solution	method
38	4	9	40	24	367,531	367,326	**366,872**	**366,848**	PGCA→IVND
39	4	10	40	24	305,729	305,363	**305,172**	**305,053**	PGCA→IVND
Average					263,529	263,399	263,199.8	260,677.1	
Avg. computing time					2.67s	26.7s			

Note. Boldface type denotes previous best solution; underline type denotes better solution; Boldface&underline denotes the new best solution.

Table 6. Results of 40 medium-sized problems and the new best solutions

5.5. Large-sized MLLS problems

Next, we ran $IVND^{50}_{1000}$ algorithm on 40 large-sized MLLS benchmark problems and repeated 10 runs. We summarize the 400 results and compare them with the existing algorithms in Table 7, and show detailed results of 40 problems in Table 8.

Method	Avg. Cost	Optimality on prev. best solutions (%)	Time (m)	CPU type	Number of processors	Sources
HGA_{1000*}	40,817,600	10.00		--	1	Dellaert et all(2000)
MMAS	40,371,702	47.50		P4 1.5G	1	Pitakaso et al.(2007)
GA_{100}	41,483,590	0.00	60	P4 2.4G	1	Homberger(2008)
GA_{3000}	--	--	60	P4 2.4G	1	Homberger(2008)
PGAI	41,002,743	0.00	60	P4 2.4G	30	Homberger(2008)
PGAC	39,809,739	52.50	60	P4 2.4G	30	Homberger(2008)
$IVND^{50}_{1000}$(Avg. of 10)	40,051,638	65.00	4.44	NB 1.6G	1	IVND
$IVND^{50}_{1000}$(Min. of 10)	39,869,210	70.00	44.4	NB 1.6G	1	IVND
Prev. best solution	39,792,241	--	--	--	--	--
New best solution	39,689,769	--	--	--	-	--

Table 7. Comparing IVND with existing algorithms on 40 large-sized problems

It can be observed from Table 7 and Table 8 that the IVND algorithm shows its best optimality among all existing algorithms since 70% of these 40 problems were found new best solution by IVND algorithm. The average computing time for each problem used by IVND algorithm was relatively low. However, four problems, i.e., problem 19, 15, 25, and 50, used much long time to finish their calculation because the interdependencies among items are relatively high for these four problems. The column *Inter D.* in Table 8 is the maximum number of affected items when the lot-size of end-product is changed.

Instance				IVND$_{1000}$			Prev. best known	New best known	New source
	I	P	Inter D.	Avg. of 10	Min. of 10	Time (m)			
0	500	36	500	597,940	597,560	6.3	**595,792**	**595,792**	PGAC
1	500	36	500	817,615	816,507	6.8	**816,058**	**816,058**	HGA
2	500	36	500	929,097	927,860	6.4	**911,036**	**911,036**	PGAC
3	500	36	500	945,317	944,626	6.2	**942,650**	**942,650**	MMAS
4	500	36	500	1,146,946	**1,145,980**	6.5	**1,149,005**	**1,145,980**	MMAS→IVND
5	500	36	11036	7,725,323	**7,689,434**	71.9	**7,812,794**	**7,689,434**	PGAC→IVND
6	500	36	3547	3,928,108	**3,923,336**	22.5	**4,063,248**	**3,923,336**	MMAS→IVND
7	500	36	1034	2,724,472	2,713,496	17.2	**2,704,332**	**2,703,004**	HGA→IVND
8	500	36	559	1,898,263	1,886,812	10.3	**1,943,809**	**1,865,141**	PGAC→IVND
9	500	36	341	1,511,600	1,505,392	6.0	**1,560,030**	**1,502,371**	MMAS→IVND
10	500	36	193607	59,911,520	**59,842,858**	179.9	**59,866,085**	**59,842,858**	PGAC→IVND
11	500	36	22973	13,498,853	**13,441,692**	58.6	**13,511,901**	**13,441,692**	PGAC→IVND
12	500	36	3247	4,751,464	**4,731,818**	34.4	**4,828,331**	**4,731,818**	PGAC→IVND
13	500	36	914	2,951,232	2,937,914	18.6	**2,910,203**	**2,910,203**	HGA
14	500	36	708	1,759,976	1,750,611	8.9	**1,791,700**	**1,740,397**	MMAS→IVND
15	500	36	1099608	472,625,159	472,088,128	106.1	**471,325,517**	**471,325,517**	PGAC
16	500	36	24234	18,719,243	**18,703,573**	80.5	**18,750,600**	**18,703,573**	MMAS→IVND
17	500	36	7312	7,321,985	**7,292,340**	33.7	**7,602,730**	**7,292,340**	MMAS→IVND
18	500	36	1158	3,592,086	**3,550,994**	23.4	**3,616,968**	**3,550,994**	PGAC→IVND
19	500	36	982	2,326,390	2,293,131	13.8	**2,358,460**	**2,291,093**	MMAS→IVND
20	500	52	500	1,189,599	1,188,210	22.4	**1,187,090**	**1,187,090**	MMAS
21	500	52	500	1,343,567	**1,341,412**	14.9	**1,341,584**	**1,341,412**	HGA→IVND
22	500	52	500	1,403,822	1,402,818	8.7	**1,400,480**	**1,384,263**	MMAS→IVND
23	500	52	500	1,386,667	1,384,263	9.1	**1,382,150**	**1,382,150**	MMAS
24	500	52	500	1,660,879	**1,658,156**	8.8	**1,660,860**	**1,658,156**	MMAS→IVND
25	500	52	11036	12,845,438	12,777,577	117.7	**13,234,362**	**12,776,833**	PGAC→IVND
26	500	52	3547	7,292,728	**7,246,237**	27.7	**7,625,325**	**7,246,237**	PGAC→IVND

Instance				IVND$_{1000}$			Prev. best known	New best known	New source
	I	P	Inter D.	Avg. of 10	Min. of 10	Time (m)			
27	500	52	1034	4,253,400	4,231,896	21.9	**4,320,868**	**4,199,064**	PGAC→IVND
28	500	52	559	2,905,006	2,889,328	10.7	**2,996,500**	**2,864,526**	MMAS→IVND
29	500	52	341	2,198,534	**2,186,429**	7.8	**2,277,630**	**2,186,429**	MMAS→IVND
30	500	52	193607	103,535,103	103,237,091	297.4	**102,457,238**	**102,457,238**	PGAC
31	500	52	22973	18,160,129	18,104,424	49.4	**18,519,760**	**18,097,215**	PGAC→IVND
32	500	52	3247	6,932,353	**6,905,070**	44.3	**7,361,610**	**6,905,070**	MMAS→IVND
33	500	52	914	4,109,712	4,095,109	41.1	**4,256,361**	**4,080,792**	PGAC→IVND
34	500	52	708	2,602,841	2,573,491	20.5	**2,672,210**	**2,568,339**	MMAS→IVND
35	500	52	1099608	768,067,039	762,331,081	121.4	**756,980,807**	**756,980,807**	PGAC
36	500	52	24234	33,393,240	33,377,419	137.7	**33,524,300**	**33,356,750**	MMAS→IVND
37	500	52	7312	10,506,439	**10,491,324**	52.1	**10,745,900**	**10,491,324**	MMAS→IVND
38	500	52	1158	5,189,651	5,168,547	29.5	**5,198,011**	**5,120,701**	PGAC→IVND
39	500	52	982	3,406,764	3,394,470	14.3	**3,485,360**	**3,381,090**	MMAS→IVND
Average				40,051,638	39,869,210	44.4	39,792,241	39,689,769	--
Avg. computing time				4.44m	44.4m				

Note. Boldface type denotes previous best solution; underline type denotes better solution; Boldface&underline denotes the new best solution.

Table 8. Results of 40 large-sized problems and the new best solutions

5.6. The effectiveness of individual parameter of VIND

Finally, we used the 40 medium-sized problems to test parameters, i.e., P, N and K_{max}, of IVND algorithm their relation between effectiveness and computing load (using medium-sized problems is just for saving computing time). We did three experiments by varying one parameter while fixing other two parameters. First, we fixed N=200 and K_{max}=5, and increased P from 10 to 200, and repeated 10 runs for each P. Second, we fixed P=50 and K_{max}=5, and increase N from 50 to 500. thirdly, P, N were fixed to 50 and 200, and K_{max} was increased from 1 to 10. The average costs gotten by the three experiments against varied parameters are shown in Table 9. A general trend can be observed that increases parameter P, N or K_{max} will all lead to better solutions been found but at the price of more computing time. However, all the parameter may contribute less to the quality of solution when they are increased large enough. Obviously, the best effectiveness-cost combination of these parameters exists for the IVND algorithm which is a worthwhile work to do in future works, but we just set these parameters manually in our experiments.

http://dx.doi.org/10.5772/55279

P	N	K_{max}	Avg. Cost of 10 runs	Comp. time of 10 runs (s)
5	200	5	264,111	30
10	200	5	263,914	57
20	200	5	263,816	104
30	200	5	263,744	144
50	200	5	263,712	233
70	200	5	263,671	308
100	200	5	263,640	433
130	200	5	263,614	553
160	200	5	263,620	674
200	200	5	263,579	832
50	10	5	266,552	40
50	50	5	264,395	87
50	100	5	263,920	135
50	150	5	263,775	186
50	200	5	263,702	220
50	250	5	263,672	274
50	300	5	263,634	309
50	400	5	263,613	376
50	500	5	263,603	463
50	600	5	263,585	559
50	200	1	263,868	74
50	200	2	263,775	100
50	200	3	263,715	136
50	200	4	263,713	178
50	200	5	263,709	225
50	200	6	263,704	276
50	200	7	263,693	341

P	N	K_{max}	Avg. Cost of 10 runs	Comp. time of 10 runs (s)
50	200	8	263,684	420
50	200	9	263,688	527
50	200	10	263,678	567

Table 9. Experimental results of different parameters for medium-sized problem

6. Summarization

The consideration of meta-heuristic is widly used in a lot of fields. Deffirent meta-heuristic algorithms are developed for solving deffirent problems, especially combinational optimization problems. In this chapter, we discussed a special case of MLLS problem. First, the general definition of MLLS problem was described. We shown its solution structure and explained its NP completeness. Second, we reviewed the meta-heuristic algorithms which have been use to solve the MLLS problem and pointed their merits and demerits. Based on the recognition, third, we investigated those implement techniques used in the meta-heuristic algorithms for solving the MLLS problems. And two criteria of distance and range were firstly defined to evaluate the effective of those techniques. We brifly discussed the mechanisms and characteristics of the techniques by using these two criteria, and provided simulation experiments to prove the correctness of the two criteria and to explain the performance and utility of them. This is one of our contributions. Fourth, we presented a succinct and easily implemented IVND algorithm and six implemental techniques for solving the MLLS problem. The IVND algorithm was evaluated by using 176 benchmark problems of different scales (small, medium and large) from literatures. The results on 96 small-sized benchmark problems showed the IVND algorithm of good optimality; it could find 100% optimal solutions in repeated 10 runs using a very low computing time(less than 1s for each problem). Experiments on other two sets of benchmark problems (40 medium-sized problems and 40 large-sized problems) showed it good efficiency and effectiveness on solving MLLS problem with product structure complex. For the medium-sized problems, the IVND can use 10 repeated runs to reach 40% of the 40 problems of their previous known best solutions and find another 20% of new best known solutions. By more repeated runs, our IVND algorithm actually had updated 30% (12 problems) of the best known solutions, and computing efficiency was also very acceptable because the longest computing time for each problem was less than one minute. For the 40 large-sized problems, the IVND algorithm delivered even more exciting results on the quality of solution. Comparison of the best solutions achieved with the new method and those established by previous methods including HGA, MMAS, and PGA shows that the IVND algorithm with the six implemental techniques are till now among the best methods for solving MLLS problem with product structure complexity considered, not only because it is easier to be understood and implemented in practice, but more importantly, it also provides quite good solutions in very acceptable time.

http://dx.doi.org/10.5772/55279

Acknowledgements

This work is supported by the Japan Society for the Promotion of Science (JSPS) under the grant No. 24510192.

Author details

Ikou Kaku[1*], Yiyong Xiao[2] and Yi Han[3]

*Address all correspondence to: kakuikou@tcu.ac.jp

1 Department of Environmental and Information studies, Tokyo City University, Japan

2 School of Reliability and System Engineering, Beihang University, Beijing, China

3 College of Business Administration, Zhejiang University of Technology, Hangzhou, China

References

[1] Afentakis, P, Gavish, B, & Kamarkar, U. (1984). Computationally efficient optimal solutions to the lot-sizing problem in multistage assembly systems, *Management Science*, , 30, 223-239.

[2] Afentakis, P, & Gavish, B. (1986). Optimal lot-sizing algorithms for complex product structures, *Operations Research*, , 34, 237-249.

[3] Almeder, C. (2010). A hybrid optimization approach for multi-level capacitated lot-sizing problems, *European Journal of Operational Research*, , 200, 599-606.

[4] Benton, W. C, & Srivastava, R. (1985). Product structure complexity and multilevel lot sizing using alternative costing policies, *Decision Sciences*, , 16, 357-369.

[5] Blackburn, J. D, & Millen, R. A. (1985). An evaluation of heuristic performance in multi-stage lot-sizing systems, *International Journal of Production Research*, , 23, 857-866.

[6] Coleman, B. J, & Mcknew, M. A. (1991). An improved heuristic for multilevel lot sizing in material requirements planning. *Decision Sciences*, , 22, 136-156.

[7] Crowston, W. B, & Wagner, H. M. (1973). Dynamic lot size models for multi-stage assembly system, *Management Science*, , 20, 14-21.

[8] Dellaert, N, & Jeunet, J. (2000). Solving large unconstrained multilevel lot-sizing problems using a hybrid genetic algorithm, *International Journal of Production Research*, 38(5), 1083-1099.

[9] Dellaert, N, Jeunet, J, & Jonard, N. (2000). A genetic algorithm to solve the general multi-level lot-sizing problem with time-varying costs, *International Journal of Production Economics*, , 68, 241-257.

[10] Han, Y, Tang, J. F, Kaku, I, & Mu, L. F. (2009). Solving incapacitated multilevel lot-sizing problem using a particle swarm optimization with flexible inertial weight, *Computers and Mathematics with Applications*, , 57, 1748-1755.

[11] Han, Y, Kaku, I, Tang, J. F, Dellaert, N, Cai, J. H, Li, Y. L, & Zhou, G. G. (2011). A scatter search approach for uncapacitated multilevel lot-sizing problems, *International Journal of Innovative Computing, Information and Control*, 7(7), 4833-4848.

[12] Han, Y, Cai, J. H, Kaku, I, Lin, H. Z, & Guo, H. D. (2012a). A note on "a genetic algorithm for the preemptive and non-preemptive multi-mode resource-constrained project scheduling problem", *Applied Mechanics and Materials*, , 127, 527-530.

[13] Han, Y, Cai, J. H, Kaku, I, Li, Y. L, Chen, Y. Z, & Tang, J. F. (2012b). Evolutionary algorithms for solving unconstrained multilevel lot-sizing problem with series structure, *Journal of Shanghai Jiaotong University*, 17(1), 39-44.

[14] Hansen, P, & Mladenovic, N. (2001a). Variable neighborhood search: principles and applications, *European Journal of Operational Research*, 130(3), 449-467.

[15] Hansen, P, Mladenovic, N, & Perez, D. (2001b). Variable neighborhood decomposition search, *Journal of Heuristics*, , 7, 335-350.

[16] Hansen, P, & Mladenovic, N. and Pe´rez J. A. M., (2008). Variable neighborhood search, *European Journal of Operational Research*, Editorial., 191, 593-595.

[17] Homberger, J. (2008). A parallel genetic algorithm for the multilevel unconstrained lot-sizing problem, *INFORMS Journal on Computing*, 20(1), 124-132

[18] Hoos, H. H, & Thomas, S. (2005). Stochastic Local Search-Foundations and Applications, Morgan Kaufmann Publishers.

[19] Kaku, I, & Xu, C. H. (2006). A soft optimization approach for solving a complicated multilevel lot-sizing problem, *in Proc. 8th Conf. Industrial Management, ICIM'200638*

[20] Kaku, I, Li, Z. S, & Xu, C. H. (2010). Solving Large Multilevel Lot-Sizing Problems with a Simple Heuristic Algorithm Based on Segmentation, *International Journal of Innovative Computing, Information and Control*, 6(3), 817-827.

[21] Mladenovic, N, & Hansen, P. (1997). Variable neighborhood search, *Computers & Operations Research*, , 24, 1097-1100.

[22] Pitakaso, R, Almeder, C, Doerner, K. F, & Hartlb, R. F. ant system for unconstrained multi-level lot-sizing problems, *Computer & Operations Research*, , 34, 2533-2552.

[23] Raza, A. S, & Akgunduz, A. (2008). A comparative study of heuristic algorithms on Economic Lot Scheduling Problem, *Computers and Industrial Engineering.* 55(1), 94-109.

[24] Steinberg, E, & Napier, H. A. (1980). Optimal multilevel lot sizing for requirements planning systems, *Management Science*, 26(12), 1258-1271.

[25] Tang, O. (2004). Simulated annealing in lot sizing problems, *International Journal of Production Economics*, , 88, 173-181.

[26] Veral, E. A. and LaForge R. L., (1985). The performance of a simple incremental lot-sizing rule in a multilevel inventory environment, *Decision Sciences*, , 16, 57-72.

[27] Xiao, Y. Y, Kaku, I, Zhao, X. H, & Zhang, R. Q. (2011a). A variable neighborhood search based approach for uncapacitated multilevel lot-sizing problems, *Computers & Industrial Engineering*, , 60, 218-227.

[28] Xiao, Y. Y, Zhao, X. H, Kaku, I, & Zhang, R. Q. (2011b). A reduced variable neighborhood search algorithm for uncapacitated multilevel lot-sizing problems, *European Journal of Operational Research, 214*, 223-231.

[29] Xiao, Y. Y, Zhao, X. H, Kaku, I, & Zhang, R. Q. (2012). Neighborhood search techniques for solving uncapacitated multilevel lot-sizing problems, *Computers & Operations Research*, 57((3)

[30] Yelle, L. E. (1979). Materials requirements lot sizing: a multilevel approach, *International Journal of Production Research*, , 17, 223-232.

[31] Zhangwill, W. I. (1968). Minimum concave cost flows in certain network, *Management Science*, , 14, 429-450.

[32] Zhangwill, W. I. (1969). A backlogging model and a multi-echelon model of a dynamic economic lot size production system-a network approach, *Management Science*, , 15, 506-527.

Chapter 5

A Two-Step Optimisation Method for Dynamic Weapon Target Assignment Problem

Cédric Leboucher, Hyo-Sang Shin, Patrick Siarry,
Rachid Chelouah, Stéphane Le Ménec and
Antonios Tsourdos

Additional information is available at the end of the chapter

http://dx.doi.org/10.5772/53606

1. Introduction

The weapon target assignment (WTA) problem has been designed to match the Command & Control (C2) requirement in military context, of which the goal is to find an allocation plan enabling to treat a specific scenario in assigning available weapons to oncoming targets. The WTA always get into situation weapons defending an area or assets from an enemy aiming to destroy it. Because of the uniqueness of each situation, this problem must be solved in real-time and evolve accordingly to the aerial/ground situation. By the past, the WTA was solved by an operator taking all the decisions, but because of the complexity of the modern warfare, the resolution of the WTA in using the power of computation is inevitable to make possible the resolution in real time of very complex scenarii involving different type of targets. Nowadays, in most of the C2 this process is designed in order to be as a support for a human operator and in helping him in the decision making process. The operator will give its final green light to proceed the intervention.

The WTA arouses a great interest among the researcher community and many methods have been proposed to cope with this problem. Besides, the WTA has been proved to be NP-complete [1]. There are two families of WTA: the Static WTA (SWTA) and the Dynamic WTA (DWTA). In both of these problems, the optimality of one solution is based either on the minimisation of the target survival after the engagement or the maximisation of the survivability of the defended assets. The main feature of the SWTA stands in its single stage approach. It is considered that all the information about the situations are provided and the problem can be considered as a constrained resource assignment problem. In contrast, the DWTA is a multi-stage problem in which the result of each stage is assessed, then use to update the aerial situation for the upcoming stages. The DWTA can also be expressed as a succession of SWTA, but the optimality of the final solution cannot be guaranteed since it comes to the same as in a greedy optimisation process. One other difference stands in the temporal dimension of the DWTA which does not exist in the SWTA. The weapons can intervene within a certain defined time because of physical, technical and operational constraints. In addition, any DWTA problem has to be solved in using real-time oriented method. By real-time it is assumed that the proposed method has to be fast enough to provide an engagement solution before the oncoming targets reached their goals. Most of the previous work on the WTA was focused on the resolution of the SWTA. Hosein and Athans was among the first to defined a cost function based on the assets [2]. This model was reused in [3] and [4]. Later, a second modelling has been proposed by Karasakal in [5], aiming to maximise the probability to suppress all the oncoming targets. One other variant of the WTA is to take into account a *threatening* value to each target according to its features and the importance of the protected assets. The research of Johansson and Falkman in [6] proposed a good overview of all the possible modelling, taking into account both of the developed models and enabling to take into consideration the value of the defended assets and the threatening index of the incoming target. Kwon *et al.* explored further this principle in assigning a value to the weapon in [7]. The main researches on the SWTA started around the 1950's. Most of the proposals to solve this problem was based on the classic optimisation processes: branch and bound algorithm appears in the survey conducted in 2006 by Cai *et al.* [8]. With the evolution of the new technologies, some more complex methods appeared in [9] in using the neural networks. The genetic algorithms are used in [4], [10] and [11] to solve the SWTA. Cullenbine is using the Tabu Search method in [12]. A different approach angle is used in [13]. In this former approach the WTA problem is treated as a resources management problem and the reactivity of the proposed approach, based on the Tabu Search, was able to deal with real-time requirement. Nowadays, this method is used in many military systems like Rapid Anti-Ship Missile-Integrated Defense System (RAIDS) [14] [13]. Whereas the SWTA had aroused the interest of the researchers first, lately the DWTA had attracted much more attention. The first DWTA was proposed by Hosein and Athans around 1990 [15]. In the proposed approach of Hosein and Athans, a sub-optimal solution was studied in order to determine a solution which was considered as "good enough" [15]. Later they developed exact methods to solve some simplified DWTA [16] [17]. The dynamic programming enables to solve the DWTA in [18], but under the assumption that all the engaged targets are destroyed. Despite its study to decrease the computational time, the problem was still treated in exponential complexity [18]. A more complex DWTA model is designed by Wu *et al.* in [19] where the temporal dimension is included under the form of firing time windows.

The studied DWTA in this chapter slightly differs from the common defined DWTA in the literature. The proposed model has been designed to fit a specific requirement from industrial application. Whereas the classic problem is considering a multi-stage approach, the solved problem considers a continuous time where the targets are evolving in the space according to their own objectives and features. The targets trajectories are designed in using Bezier's curves defined by 4 control points which the last one is set to the centre of area that we are defending. The choice of this trajectory modelling has been done in order to add more diversity in the tested scenarii. The current situation is updated in real time, which means that the proposed algorithm must be as reactive as possible to cope with the oncoming targets. In order to solve the presented problem in the fastest and the most accurate way, a two-step optimisation method is proposed. The first step optimise the assignment of the

http://dx.doi.org/10.5772/53606

weapons to the targets, then the optimal firing sequence is obtained in using the results obtained from the first step. The optimal assignment is determined in using the graph theory, and more especially the Hungarian method in a bipartite graph. The used of this method in the first step is motivated by the optimality and the polynomial complexity of the method. Then, the computation of the firing sequence is optimised in using a particle swarm optimisation (PSO) process combined to the evolutionary game theory (EGT). This former method has been proved as efficient in general allocation resources problem [20].

The performance index for the evaluation of the assignment is determined by three different criteria: the capacity to propose an early fire, the width of the firing time window and the minimisation of the overflying of the defended area by our own assets for security purpose. The quality of the firing sequence is obtained from the reactivity of the algorithm to treat the targets in the earliest possible way, the respect of the system constraints and the avoidance of idle time when a firing is possible.

The goal of this chapter is to develop an efficient method to solve a target based DWTA problem involving technical and operational constraints. A mission is considered as achieve only if no targets reach the defending area. The contribution of this paper includes the following aspects:

- Design of a DWTA model taking into account target trajectories and operational and technical constraints on the weapons.
- A two-step approach based on the graph theory, then a combined swarm intelligence and evolutionary game method to solve the DWTA in an optimised fashion.
- The reducing computational load in order to enable real-time applications.
- The targets are following a Bezier's curve trajectory in order to sow the confusion among the defending system.
- The success of one fire is determined by the draw of one random number in $[0,1]$, then compared to a probability threshold of kill (PK).

The rest of this chapter is organised as follows: the second section describes the details of the studied DWTA, the third section introduces the background of Hungarian algorithm, particle swarm optimisation and evolutionary game theory. Then the fourth section details the proposed method before testing and analysing the obtained results by using a dedicated simulator designed for this DWTA problem. The chapter ends with the conclusion of this study.

2. Background of the proposed approach

2.1. The Hungarian algorithm

The assignment problem arouses the interest of the researchers community for a while. The principle consists of finding a maximum weight matching in a weighted bipartite graph. It is more commonly formulated as: there are two distinct sets, one contain agents, the other one contain tasks. Note that each agent has his own ability to realise a job properly and this capability is represented by a quantitative value. The global objective to assign all the agents to the jobs can be achieved in one optimal way. The Hungarian method published by

Kuhn in 1955 is inspired by the work of two Hungarian researchers: Dénes Kõnig and Jenõ Egervàry [21]. This method has been proved as optimal and polynomial.

Let G be a complete bipartite graph composed, one hand by a set of $|A|$ agents and one other hand by $|T|$ tasks. Then $G = (A, T, E)$, where E denotes the set of the edges linking the set of Agents with the set of Tasks. Note that each edge from E is weighted by a positive cost $c(i, j)$, where $i \in \{1, \ldots, |A|\}$ and $j \in \{1, \ldots, |T|\}$. The function $P : (A \cup T) \longrightarrow \mathbb{R}$ represents the potential if $p(i) + p(j) \leq c(i, j)$ for each $i \in A$ and $j \in T$. The potential value is obtained in summing all the potential from the set $A \cup T$: $p = \sum_{v \in (A \cup T)} p(v)$. The Hungarian method enables to find the perfect matching and the potential equalising the cost and the value, which means that both of them are optimal.

2.2. The particle swarm optimisation

Kennedy and Eberhart [22], the founders of the PSO method, was inspired by the behaviour of animals acting in society to achieve a goal. For example, the birds, the fishes, etc. can make up a very efficient collective intelligence in exchanging very basic information about the environment in which they are evolving. From this starting point, the authors have designed the PSO method to solve many optimisation problems over the last few decades. A swarm is composed of particles (representing a solution) flying on the solution space and communicating with the neighbourhood the quality of the current position.

The first step in PSO algorithm is to define the moving rules on the solution space for the particles. Let $X_i^t = [x_{i1}^t, x_{i2}^t, \ldots, x_{iD}^t,]$, $x_{id}^t \in \{0, 1\}$ be a particle in a population of P particles and composed of D dimensions. The velocity of this particle is denoted as $V_i^t = [v_{i1}^t, v_{i2}^t, \ldots, v_{iD}^t,]$, $v_{id}^t \in \mathbb{R}$. Then, as in the PSO method described in [23], the next step is to define the best position for the particle $P_i^t = [p_{i1}^t, p_{i2}^t, \ldots, p_{iD}^t,]$, $p_{id}^t \in \mathbb{R}$, and the best position $P_g^t = [p_{g1}^t, p_{g2}^t, \ldots, p_{gD}^t,]$, $p_{gd}^t \in \mathbb{R}$ of the entire population at the iteration t. The velocity of the particle i is adjusted in respect to the direction d with:

$$v_{id}^{t+1} = \omega_1 v_{id}^t + \omega_2(x(t) - x_{ind}(t)) + \omega_3(x(t) - x_{global}(t)).$$

The parameter ω_1 denotes the weight of the particle inertia. ω_2 is the coefficient associated to the individual coefficient. Then, ω_3 denotes the social coefficient. The final step of one PSO iteration is to update the position of the particles in using the following formula:

$$X_i^{t+1} = X_i^t + V_i^t.$$

This process enables to find an optimal solution in repeating this process. In the classical version of the PSO [24], these coefficients are drawn randomly in order to maximise the exploration of the solution space by the particles. It can be a weakness when the computational time has to be the shortest possible. The studied method proposes to decrease this computational time in using the Evolutionary Game Theory (EGT) to determine the three coefficients ω_1, ω_2 and ω_3. Since the particles are "jumping" on the solution space, the creators wished to limit the jumped distance to a maximum length determined by the value of V_{max} usually determined with respect to the solution space.

http://dx.doi.org/10.5772/53606

2.3. The evolutionary game theory

The evolutionary game theory appeared initially in a biologic context. The need to model the evolution phenomena led to the use of mathematical theory of the games to explain the strategic aspect of the evolution. Over the last few decades, the EGT has aroused interest of the economists, sociologists, social scientists, as well as the philosophers. Although the evolutionary game theory found its origin in biologic science, such an expansion to different fields can be explained by three facts. First of all, the notion of evolution has to be understood as the change of beliefs and norms over time. Secondly, the modelling of strategies change provides a social aspect which matches exactly the social system interactions. Finally, it was important to model dynamically the interactions within a population, which was one of the missing elements of the classic game theory. As in this former domain, the evolutionary game theory deals with the equilibrium which is a key point in both of the theories. Here the equilibrium point is called the evolutionary stable strategy. The principle of the EGT is not only based on the strategy performance obtained by itself, but also the performance obtained in the presence of the others.

2.3.1. Evolutionary Stable Strategies

An Evolutionary Stable Strategy (ESS) is a strategy such that, if all members of a population adopt it, then no mutant strategy could invade the population under the influence of natural selection. Assume we have a mixed population consisting of mostly p^* individuals (agents playing optimal strategy p^*) with a few individuals using strategy p. That is, the strategy distribution in the population is:

$$(1-\varepsilon)p^* + \varepsilon p$$

where $\varepsilon > 0$ is the small frequency of p users in the population. Let the fitness, i.e. payoff of an individual using strategy q in this mixed population, be

$$\pi(q, (1-\varepsilon)p^* + \varepsilon p).$$

Then, an interpretation of Maynard Smith's requirement [25] for p^* to be an ESS is that, for all $p \neq p^*$,

$$\pi(p, (1-\varepsilon)p^* + \varepsilon p) > \pi(p^*, (1-\varepsilon)p^* + \varepsilon p)$$

for all $\varepsilon > 0$ "sufficiently small", for agents minimizing their fitness.

2.3.2. Replicator dynamics

A common way to describe strategy interactions is using matrix games. Matrix games are described using notations as follows. e_i is the ith unit line vector for $i = 1, ..., m$.

$A_{ij} = \pi(e_i, e_j)$ is the $m \times m$ payoff matrix.

$\Delta^m \equiv \{p = (p_1, ..., p_m) \mid p_1 + ... + p_m = 1,\ 0 \leq p_i \leq 1\}$ is the set of mixed strategies (probability distributions over the pure strategies e_i).

Then, $\pi(p, q) = p \cdot Aq^T$ is the payoff of agents playing strategy p facing agents playing strategy q.

Another interpretation is $\pi(p,q)$ being the fitness of a large population of agents playing pure strategies (p describing the agent proportion in each behaviour inside a population) with respect to a large q population.

The replicator equation (RE) is an Ordinary Differential Equation expressing the difference between the fitness of a strategy and the average fitness in the population. Lower payoffs (agents are minimizers) bring faster reproduction in accordance with Darwinian natural selection process.

$$\dot{p}_i = -p_i(e_i \cdot Ap^T - p \cdot Ap^T)$$

RE for $i = 1, ..., m$ describes the evolution of strategy frequencies p_i. Moreover, for every initial strategy distribution $p(0) \in \delta^m$, there is an unique solution $p(t) \in \delta^m$ for all $t \geq 0$ that satisfies the replicator equation. The replicator equation is the most widely used evolutionary dynamics. It was introduced for matrix games by Taylor and Jonker [26].

Note that this introducing to the EGT and the PSO comes from one of our previous study in [20].

3. The formulation of the DWTA: A target-based model

A common approach to the DWTA problem based on the capabilities of the defence system to minimise the probability that a target can leak the proposed engagement plan. However, the problem dealt with in this study is slightly different from the classic DWTA. Whereas the classic DWTA is considering a multi-stage approach, the solved problem considers a continuous time where the targets are evolving in the space according to their own objectives and features. The proposed model has been designed to fit a specific requirement from industrial application, which explains this different approach.

The weapon system is defending an area from oncoming targets. This area is represented by a circle. All the weapons are disposed randomly within this range. In order to make the problem as general as possible, it is assumed that each weapon has its own velocity and own range. The targets are aiming the centre of the area to defend. The trajectories of the targets are designed by Bezier's curves in using 4 control points, all randomly drawn on the space, but the last point which is set to the centre of the area to defend. Thus, the problem presents a high diversity and can test the proposed method in the most of possible tricky cases. It is also assumed that the velocity of the targets and of the weapons are constant.

The assignment and the firing time sequence are computed in real-time in order to validate the reactivity of the studied algorithm. Which means that a timer is set at the beginning of the simulation, and the position of the targets evolves accordingly to this time.

3.1. The engagement plan

The engagement plan represents the solution space. An engagement plan is composed of one assignment weapon/target and completed by a date to fire. For example, if the following situation involves 3 weapons and 2 targets, a possible engagement plan EP could be:

$$EP(t) = \{(W_1, T_2, t + FT_1); (W_3, T_1, t + FT_3)\}$$

Where t denotes the simulation time and the W_i, $i \in \{1,2,3\}$ and T_j, $j \in \{1,2\}$ represent the weapon i and the target j. The variable FT_i denotes the Firing Time computed for the weapon i. The engagement plan evolves accordingly to the situation and depends on the current simulation time and on the aerial situation. In this application, the engagement plan is recomputed every P seconds in order to make up a very reactive engagement plan capable of dealing with the trickier cases in which the targets are constantly changing their trajectories.

3.2. The choice of a two-step optimisation method

Since the complexity of the presented problem grows exponentially with the number of targets and weapons, to design an algorithm capable of handling the real-time computation, but taking into account very diversified performance indexes, the choice of two different steps was natural. Lloyd [1] proved that the DWTA is a NP-complete problem. Therefore, it is hard to find an exact optimisation method capable of solving the DWTA problem in an exact way within a reasonable time. The reasonable time implies a high frequency which can enable the real-time application of the optimisation method. Note that the system must be able to provide results in real-time in the DWTA problem since the engagement changes as the targets keep evolving in the aerial space during the computation. With these reasons, using a heuristic approach providing suboptimal solutions in real-time could be the best way to handle the DWTA problem. One other problem is to be able to quantify the quality of one proposed solution: the performance index of the assignment, and the firing sequence cannot be evaluated in using the same performance criterion. Whereas the assignment is evaluated from the system point of view, the firing sequence is evaluated from the weapons features. Dividing the problem into two parts could lead to the modification of the solution space and the optimum solution could be not the same as the optimal one if the entire solution space was considered. However regarding the real-time computation, and the heterogeneity of the considered criteria, dividing this problem into two steps makes sense in terms of reality and applicability of the designed model, and in terms of quality of the found solution.

3.3. The weapon-target assignment

In order to assign the targets to the available weapons, the Hungarian algorithm is used. The weapons and the targets are modelled as an asymmetric bipartite graph. The Figure 1 shows an example of possible assignment graph used. In the studied problem, it is assumed that the initial number of weapons is greater than the number of oncoming targets.

The quality of the proposed assignment is evaluated according to three different criteria: the capacity to propose an early fire, the width of the firing time window and the minimisation of the overflying of the defended area by our own assets for security purpose. These criteria respectively represent:

- the capability of the system to propose an early firing date, and then its ability to cope with a target in the earliest possible date in order to avoid any risk.
- the width of the firing time windows represents the time that we have to cope with one target, then the larger is this firing time windows, the more time we have to propose one engagement solution,

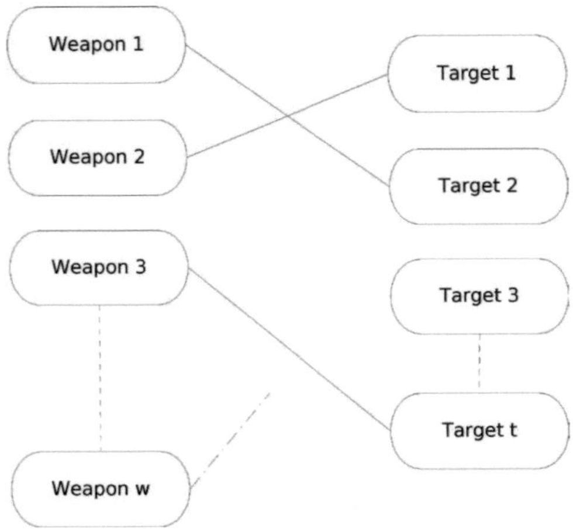

Figure 1. Example of asymmetric bipartite graph with w weapons and t targets

- limiting the overfly in our own area enables to cope with security problem in case of material failure.

3.4. The sequencing of the firing time

As soon as the weapons are assigned to the targets, the sequencing of the firing is computed with respect to the weapons properties (range, velocity) and the firing time windows as well.

In order to evaluate the quality of the proposed solution, the performance index is based on the reactivity of the algorithm, the respect of the system constraints and the avoidance of idle time when a firing is possible.

The system is subject to some technical constraints as a required time between two firing times, which depends on the system. In the designed simulator this time is fixed to 3 seconds.

3.5. Mathematical modelling

This section describes the mathematical modelling of each step followed to achieve the DWTA. The first step is the assignment of the targets to the weapons, and then the sequencing of the firing time to complete in the best possible way the destroying of all the threatening targets. The weapon-target assignment is done by using the graph theory, especially the Hungarian algorithm. The second part is done by integrating two approaches: the PSO and the EGT to make up an efficient real-time oriented algorithm to solve the firing sequence problem.

In the following section, $FTW_{w/t}$ denotes the set of the firing time windows (time windows in which a weapon w can be fired with a given probability to reach the target t). $EFF_{w/t}$ denotes the earliest feasible fire for the weapon w on the target t. The latest feasible fire for the weapon w on the target t is denoted by $LFF_{w/t}$. $E_{w/t}$ represents the edge linking the weapon w with the target t. The average speed of the weapon w is denoted by S_w. R_t and R_w denote the state of the target t (respectively the weapon w). The states are composed of the

http://dx.doi.org/10.5772/53606

(x_t, y_t) position and the speed (v_{t_x}, v_{t_y}) of the target t (respectively (x_w, y_w) position and the speed (v_{w_x}, v_{w_y}) of the weapon w) in the (x, O, y) plan. The entering point of the target t in the capture zone of the weapon w and the entering point of the defended area is computed in the same time as the $FTW_{w/t}$ and they are denoted by $P_{t_{in}}$ and $P_{t_{out}}$. The initial position of the weapon w is denoted by $P_{w_0} = (x_{w_0}, y_{w_0})$.

3.5.1. The assignment part: Hungarian algorithm

Let W be the set of the available weapons and T the set of the oncoming targets. If A represents the assignments linking the vertices W to the targets T. $G = (W, T, A)$ denotes the complete bipartite graph.

The weight of each edge is computed from the linear combination of the three criteria: earliest possible fire, width of the firing time windows and minimising the overfly of the defended area. These criteria are represented as follows:

$$f_1(E_{w/t}) = EFF_{w/t}, (w \in W), (t \in T)$$

As mentioned, $EFF_{w/t}$ denotes the earliest feasible fire for the weapon w on the target t.

$$f_2(E_{w/t}) = LFF_{w/t} - EFF_{w/t}, (w \in W), (t \in T)$$

$EFF_{w/t}$ denotes the earliest feasible fire for the weapon w on the target t. The latest feasible fire for the weapon w on the target t is denoted by $LFF_{w/t}$.

$$f_3(E_{w/t}) = d\left(P_{t_{out}}, P_{w_0}\right)$$

Here the function $d(P_1, P_2)$ represents the Euclidean distance function between the point P_1 and the point P_2. This criterion is shown in the Figure 2.

Then, the global weight of the assignment $E_{w/t}$ is the linear combination of the three functions described above: $H(E_{w/t}) = \alpha_1 f_1(E_{w/t}) + \alpha_2 f_2(E_{w/t}) + \alpha_3 f_3(E_{w/t})$, where $H(E_{w/t})$ denotes the weighting function of the assignment $E_{w/t}$ and $(\alpha_1, \alpha_2, \alpha_3) \in [0,1]^3$, with $\alpha_1 + \alpha_2 + \alpha_3 = 1$.

The cost matrix used for the Hungarian algorithm has the following form:

$$H = \begin{pmatrix} E_{1/1} & E_{2/1} & E_{3/1} & \cdots & E_{|W|/1} \\ E_{1/2} & E_{2/2} & E_{3/2} & \cdots & E_{|W|/2} \\ \vdots & \vdots & \vdots & \cdots & \vdots \\ E_{1/|T|} & E_{2/|T|} & E_{3/|T|} & \cdots & E_{|W|/|T|} \end{pmatrix}$$

$|T|$ and $|W|$ represent the cardinal of the sets T and W.

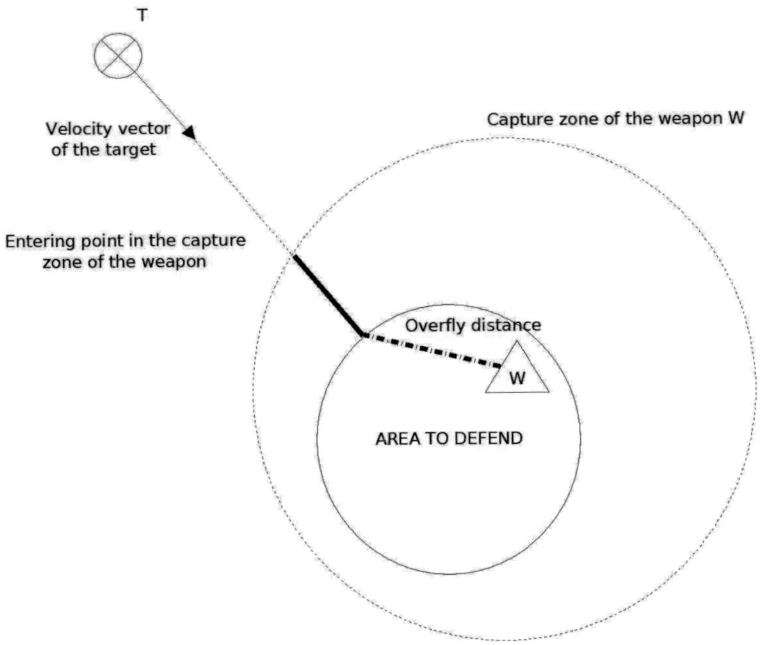

Figure 2. Representation of the overflying criterion. The used value is the Euclidean distance between the entering point of the target in the area to defend and the initial position of the weapon.

3.5.2. The firing time sequencing: EGPSO

As described in the section 2.2, the EGPSO process is based on the combination of the PSO algorithm combined to the EGT in order to increase the convergence speed [27]. In this section, $FS = [FT_i], i = \{1, \ldots, w\}$ denotes a firing sequence for the w selected weapons from the previous assignment and FT_i represents the firing time of the weapon i ($i \leq |W|$). In the proposed model, FS represents one particle composed by the set of the firing times for each weapon. Since the solution space is composed by the firing time windows, it can be very heterogeneous in terms of length along each dimension. In order to avoid an unequal exploration of the solution space, the normalisation over the solution space is operated. Thus, the solution space is reduced to a $[0, 1]^{|W|}$ hypercube and enables a homogeneous exploring by the particles.

In order to evaluate the performance of a proposed solution, the global performance index is based on the reactivity of the algorithm, the respect of the system constraints and the avoidance of idle time when a firing is possible. The global cost function is obtained in multiplying each criterion. The multiplication is selected to consider evenly all the criteria. Thus, if one criterion is not respected by the proposed engagement plan, the cost function will decrease accordingly to the unsatisfied criterion.

The first performance index based on the time delay enables to quantify the reactivity of the system in summing the firing times. The function f_1 enables to express this criterion.

http://dx.doi.org/10.5772/53606

$$f_4(FS) = \sum_{t=1}^{T} FT_t$$

Where, FT denotes the firing time of the weapon assigned to the target t.

The second criterion evaluates the feasibility of the proposed solution to respect the short time delay due to the system constraints. This criterion is based on the presence of constraint violations. When any of the constraints is violated, the proposed solution takes the maximum value in order to avoid infeasible solution.

$$f_5(FS) = \sum_{w=1}^{W} \text{Conflict}(w)$$

The vector Conflict $= [c_i]$, $i = \{1, \ldots, |W|\}$ with $c_i = 1$ if there is a constraint violation by the weapon i, otherwise $c_i = 0$.

The third and last criterion is based on the idle time of the system. This criterion enables to avoid the inactivity of the system if there are possible fires by the current time. In the best case, this value should be reduced to the time constraint multiplied by the number of available weapons.

$$f_6(FS) = \sum_{w=1}^{W-1} (FS_{w+1} - FS_w)$$

Note that the FS vector is sorted before computing this performance index function to the current particle.

When all the criteria are computed, the global performance of the proposed firing sequence is obtained as:

$$F(FS) = \begin{cases} (f_4(FS) + 1).f_6(FS) & \text{if } f_5(FS) = 0 \\ +\infty & \text{if } f_5(FS) \neq 0 \end{cases}$$

4. The proposed method

The proposed method is based on the consecutive use of the Hungarian algorithm to solve the assignment problem before determining the fire sequencing using the PSO combined with the EGT.

4.1. A two step-method

As described on the Flowchart 3, the two-step process computes first the optimal assignment of the targets to the weapons, then in a second time the optimal firing sequence is determined.

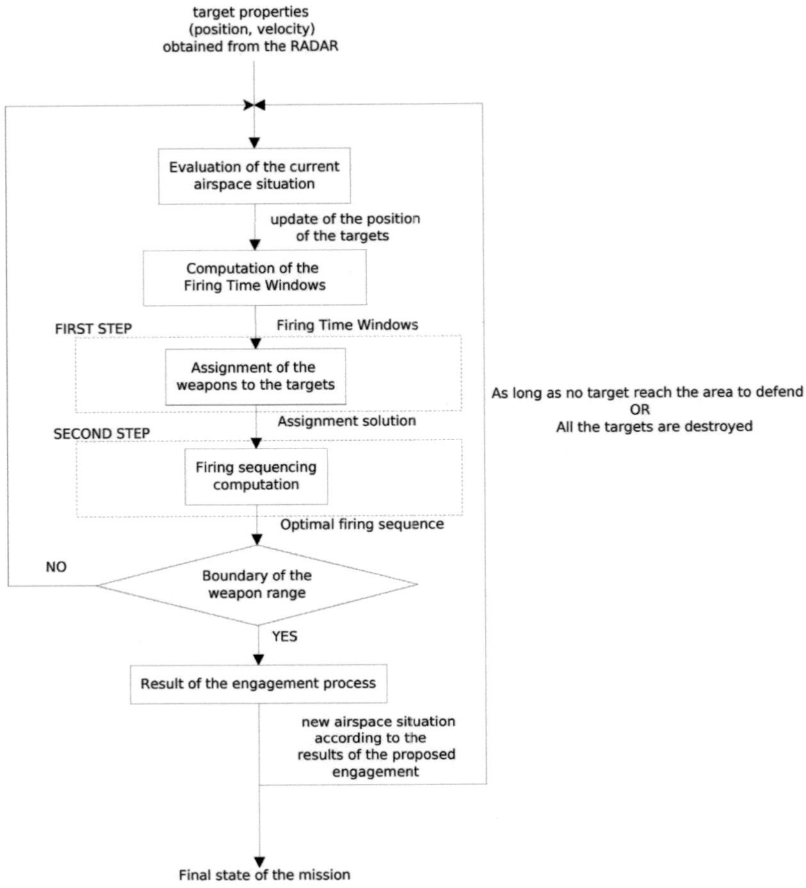

Figure 3. Representation of the two-step method to solve the DWTA.

4.2. The Hungarian algorithm

The assignment of the targets to the weapons is realised in using the Hungarian algorithm [21]. The section 3.5.1 states all the required details enabling to understand the principles of the used method. Since in real scenarii the number of targets is only rarely the same as the number of weapons, the Hungarian algorithm designed for asymmetric bipartite graphs is used. The following parameters are used to determine the best assignment: the cost matrix has a $|T| \times |W|$ form in order to assign all the targets and the coefficients of this cost matrix are determined in using the equations described in 3.5.1.

4.3. The integration of the particle swarm optimisation with the evolutionary game theory

There are two main steps in this approach, the first one is the movement of the swarm in using only, first the inertia, then only the individual component, then only the social component. From the obtained results of the movement of the three swarms, the payoff

http://dx.doi.org/10.5772/53606

matrix is composed by the mean fitness of the particles composing each swarm. Let S be the set of the available strategies s_i, $i \in \{1,2,3\}$ which are as follows:

s_1: Use of the pure strategy *inertia*

s_2: Use of the pure strategy *individual*

s_3: Use of the pure strategy *social*

After one iteration using each strategy successively, the payoff matrix consists of the mean value of the swarm. A denotes this payoff matrix:

$$\Pi = \begin{pmatrix} \pi(s_1) & \frac{\pi(s_1)+\pi(s_2)}{2} & \frac{\pi(s_1)+\pi(s_3)}{2} \\ \frac{\pi(s_2)+\pi(s_1)}{2} & \pi(s_2) & \frac{\pi(s_2)+\pi(s_3)}{2} \\ \frac{\pi(s_3)+\pi(s_1)}{2} & \frac{\pi(s_3)+\pi(s_2)}{2} & \pi(s_3) \end{pmatrix}$$

The coefficients $\pi(s_i)$, $i \in \{1,2,3\}$ are the mean value of the swarm after using the pure strategy s_i. The evolutionary game process used to converge to the evolutionary stable strategy is the *replicator dynamic* described in [20]. As soon as the population is stabilised, the proposed algorithm stop running the replicator dynamic. This ESS gives the stable strategy rate, generally composed by a mix of the strategies s_1, s_2, and s_3. Then, the final step uses these rates as coefficients in the PSO algorithm.

The principle of the method is described on the Flowchart 4 and by the following process step by step:

1. Initialisation of the swarm in position and velocity
2. For a maximum number of iterations
   (a) Random selection of particles following the classical PSO process (exploration) and the particles following the EGPSO (increase computational speed).
   (b) Classic iteration of the PSO in using only one strategy for each swarm (inertial, individual, social)
   (c) Computation of the payoff matrix in computing the mean value of the swarm in using the strategies
   (d) Find the evolutionary stable strategy depending on the payoff matrix
   (e) Classic iteration of the PSO using the previously found coefficients
   (f) Check if the swarm is stabilised
      - If YES, restart the swarm like at the step 1
      - If NOT, keep running the algorithm
3. Obtain the optimal solution

In the presented simulation, the PSO parameters are defined as:

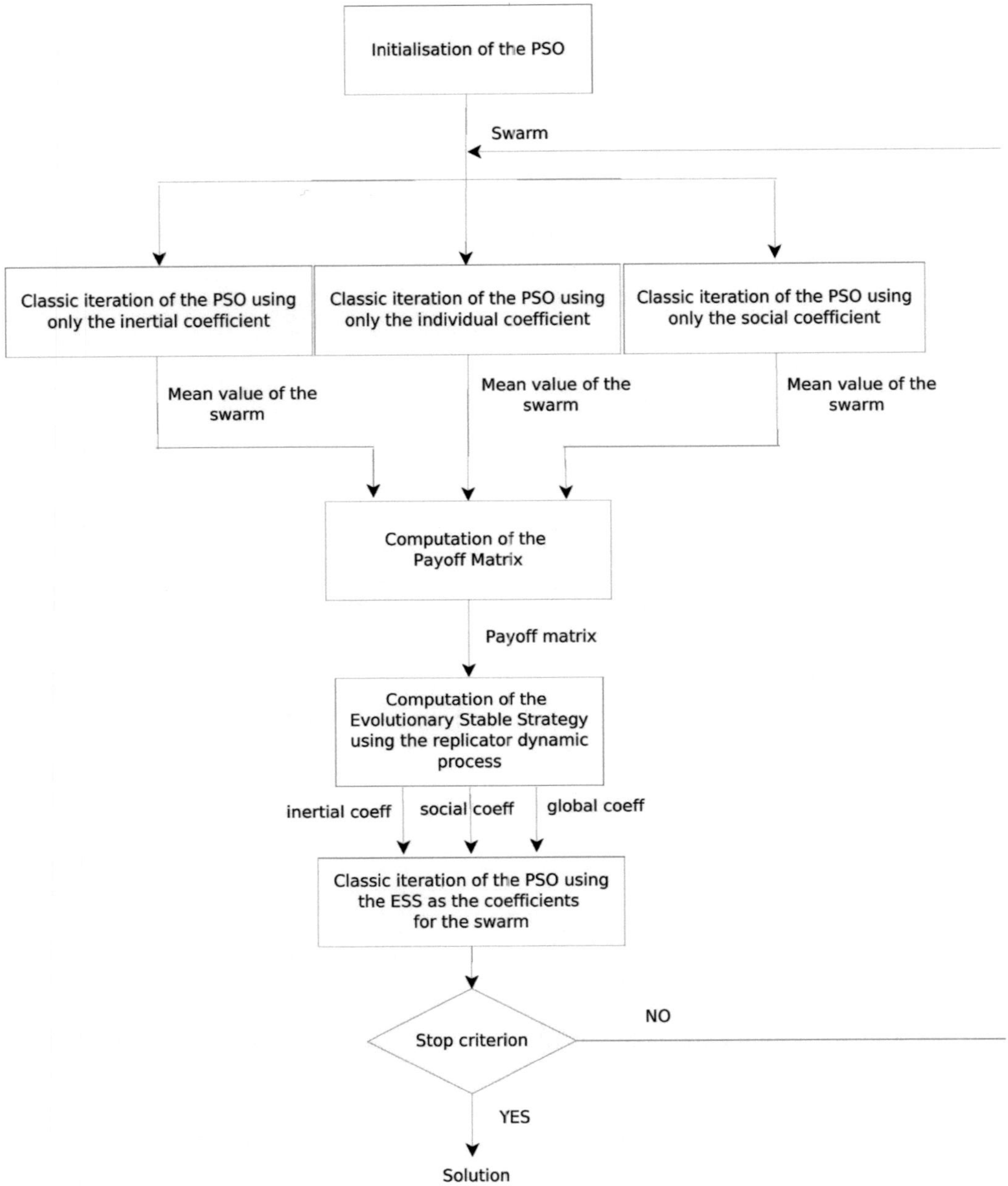

Figure 4. Details on the method designed to mix EGT and PSO.

- 50 particles are used to explore the solution space.
- The maximum distance travelled by one particle in one iteration is limited to 1/10 along each dimension. Notice that since the solution space has been normalised, the maximum velocity enables an homogeneous exploration of the solution space.
- In order to be able to be competitive in real-time, the exit criterion is a defined time of 2500 ms, after that the best found solution is considered as the optimal one.

In order to enable a quick convergence to the optimal vector rate of the PSO coefficients, the EGT process is launched in using as payoff matrix Π described in the section 4.3. The replicator equation is computed over 500 hundred generations, and then the obtained result is considered as

5. Results and comments

In this section, the efficiency of the proposed approach is analysed. After running 100 times a simulation, the number of experiences that the mission is successfully achieved is compared to the number of times it fails. Then, in a second time the evolution of the assignment is studied in analysing the target motions and the proposed engagement plan. The study ends with the analysis of the human operator point of view in order to determine if the proposed algorithm can be reliable and stable for the operator. By stable, it is assumed that the operator can have a global overview of the next engagement to execute in advance, and that this plan won't change if there are no major changes in the aerial situation (suppressed enemy or missing fire for example).

In the presented simulator, the used parameters are set up as follows:

The aerial space:
Square of 50000 m by 50000 m

Weapons
The initial position is within a radius of 3000 m around the central objective
The range of each weapon is randomly drawn between 10000 meters and 15000 meters.

Targets
The initial position is set up between 30000 m and 50000 m from the main objective located on the centre of the space.
The trajectories that the targets are following are modelled in using a Bezier curve defined by 4 control points. The last control point is automatically set as the centre of the space $(0,0)$.
The speed is randomly drawn between 50 m/s and 900 m/s.

The initial conditions:
16 Weapons vs. 12 Targets.

Condition of engagement success:
The success of an engagement one weapon on one target is determined in drawing one random number. If this number is greater than a determined value, then the shoot is considered as a success. Otherwise, it is considered that the target avoids the weapon. In this simulator this value is arbitrary fixed to 0.25, which means that the probability of operating a successful shot is 75%.

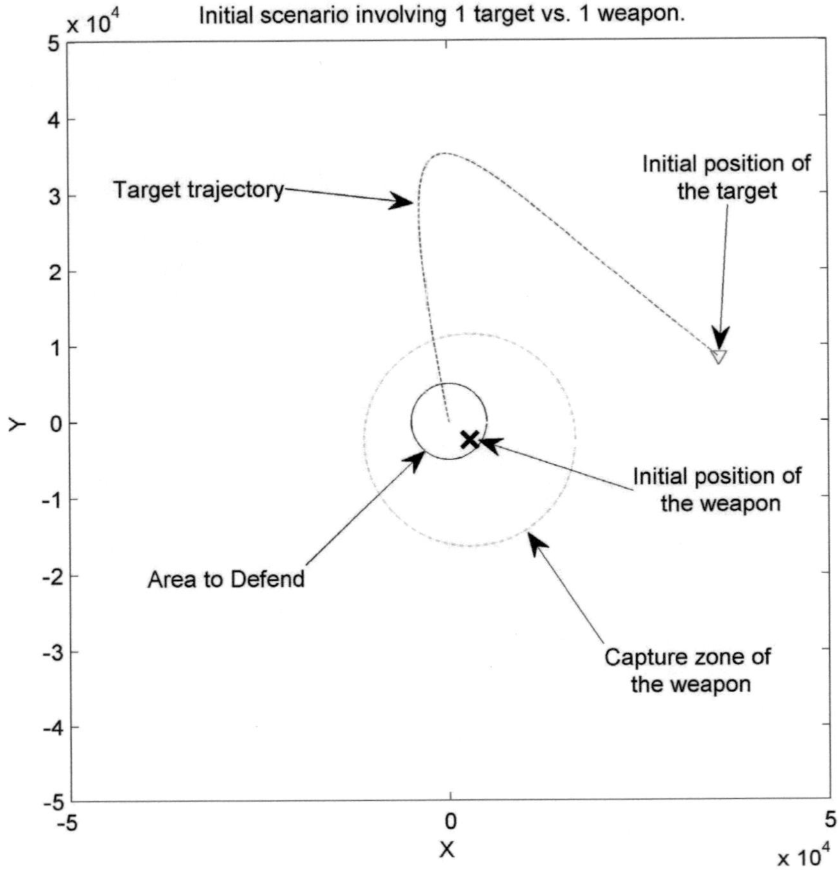

Figure 5. Representation of a possible initialisation of trajectory and weapon position. The triangle marker represents the initial position of the target. The dot line is the trajectory that the target will follow to reach its goal. The continuous line represents the area that we are defending and the cross marker surrounded by a dot line denote the defending weapon and its capture zone.

The Figure 5 shows a possible initialisation of a scenario. Note that if the trajectory is a priori known by the target, the defending side has no information at all but the final point of the target and its current position.

The analysis of the evolution of the assignment of the weapons to the oncoming targets clearly shows stability over the simulation time as long as there are no major change in the scenario. A major change in the scenario can be qualified by the suppression of one enemy which leads to the reconsideration of the entire scenario. Otherwise, the proposed method clearly shows a good stability over the simulation time which is required in the presented case. Considering the presence of a human operator having the final decision making and using this method as a help in the decision making process, it is important for the proposed engagement to be continuous over the time when the aerial situation does not vary dramatically. The upper graph of the Figure 6 displays the assignment of the target t over the number of iterations. The vertical lines identify the instants when a target has

http://dx.doi.org/10.5772/53606

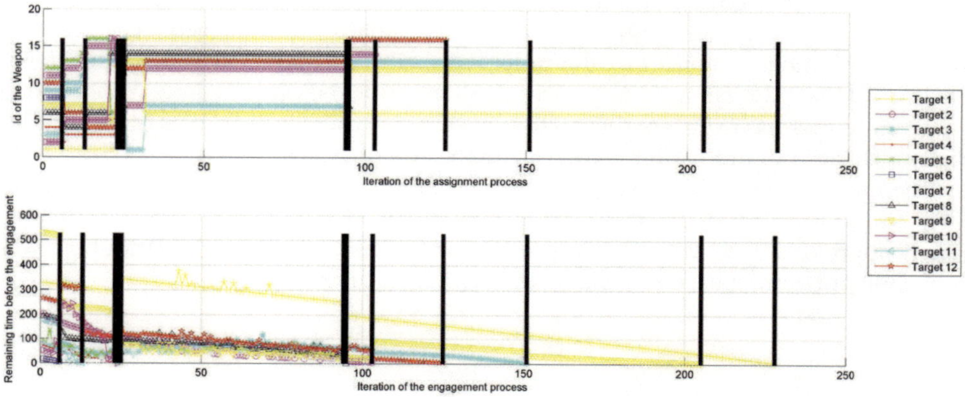

Figure 6. The upper graph illustrates the variation in the assignment process over the time. The regularity of the proposed assignment can be noticed, especially as long as the aerial situation does not change (no target are suppressed). The black vertical lines highlight these phases. The lower graph shows the evolution of the proposed firing time to engage the target over the time.

been killed, then it denotes a change in the aerial situation. During the different highlighted phases, the assignment presents some interesting features as the regularity over the time when the aerial situation keep being similar. The lower graph on the Figure 6 represents the evolution of the firing time for each target over the time. The vertical lines have the same meaning as the upper graph and denotes a change in the aerial situation like, for example, a suppressed enemy or an unsuccessful fire. This second graph highlights the continuity of the proposed firing sequence over the time. It is shown that the operator can not only approve the firing sequence in executing the firing, but the operator can follow the entire scenario and can anticipate the upcoming events. The Figure 7 focuses on the real time aspect in focusing only on the operator point of view. Indeed this Figure represents a zoom on the 25 last seconds before firing the weapons. The horizontal dash line illustrates a time limit of 5 seconds from which the operator can execute the firing.

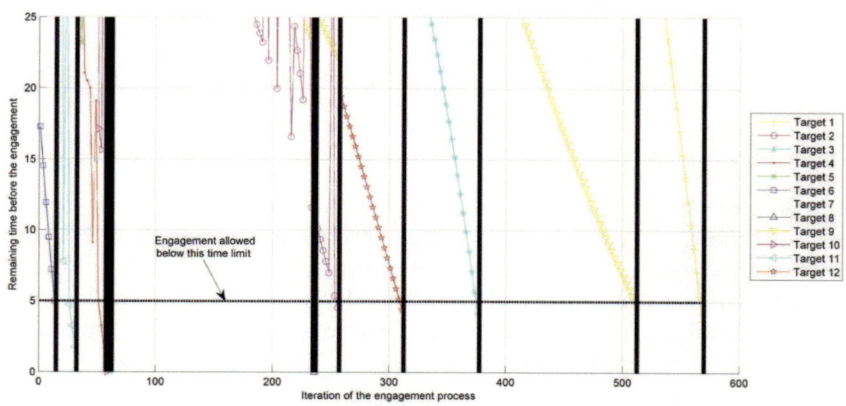

Figure 7. This graph represents a zoom on the final instruction of the operator to execute the firing of the weapon as soon as the proposed firing time is within 5 seconds of the current time. This limit is illustrated by the horizontal dash line.

In order to test the efficiency of the proposed method over different scenario, the designed experience has been launched 100 times and the final result archived. The pie diagram 8 shows the number of times that the proposed method achieved its goal versus the number of time it fails. The analysis of this result shows that the proposed algorithm successfully achieved its mission in 96% of the cases. If we look into details the causes of these failures, we can notice that 3 of the 4 failures was due to the lack of available weapons. Which means that the method does not achieved its goal because of the probability. Indeed, with PK threshold fixed to $PK = 0.90$ and 16 available weapons versus 12 targets, we have an estimate failure rate of approximatively 2 %. This last result comes from the binomial distribution, where the probability of getting exactly T success in W trials is given by:

$$P(T; W, PK) = \frac{W!}{T!(W-T)!} PK^T (1 - PK)^{W-T}$$

Thus, to solve this issue, two possible ways could be explored: first, the increasing of available weapons; second, using more accurate weapons. Although both of the proposed solutions can cope with this issue, it leads to increase the cost of the mission. Controlling this probability enables to optimise the used deployment to protect our area.

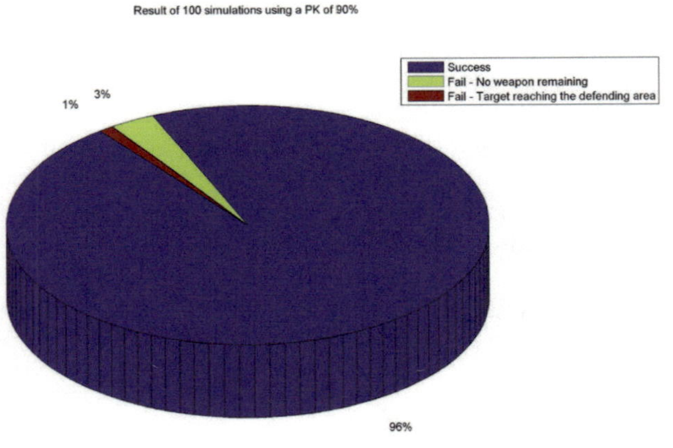

Figure 8. This bar diagram illustrates the number of time that the simulation is a success versus the number of time that it fails.

6. Conclusion

In this chapter, a two-step optimisation method for the DWTA was proposed. Based on the successive use of the Hungarian algorithm, and a PSO combined with the EGT, the proposed algorithm shows reliable results in terms of performance and real-time computation. The proposed method is verified using one simulator designed to create random scenarii and to follow the normal evolution of the battlefield in real-time. The initialised scenario was composed of 16 weapons versus 12 targets. The stability of the assignment and the continuity of the firing sequence was analysed over the launch of 100 simulations. Regarding the probability of successfully achieved the mission, a short study about the binomial distribution has been done and could be helpful in the mission planning process to determine the optimal number of available weapons before the mission. The simulation results have shown the efficiency of the proposed two-step approach in various cases. The proposed algorithm achieves its objective in 96% for the given scenarii which include random simulation parameters selected for the generality of the senarii. Note that from a probability study on this application, with the chosen simulation parameters, 2% of the scenarii was expected to be failed simply because of the associated probability laws based on a Binomial distribution.

Author details

Cédric Leboucher[1,*], Hyo-Sang Shin[2], Patrick Siarry[3], Rachid Chelouah[4], Stéphane Le Ménec[1] and Antonios Tsourdos[2]

* Address all correspondence to: cedric.leboucher@mbda-systems.com

1 MBDA France, 1 av. Reaumur, Le Plessis Robinson, France
2 Cranfield University, School of Engineering, College Road, Cranfield, Bedford, UK
3 Université Paris-Est Créteil (UPEC), LISSI (EA 3956), Créteil, France
4 L@ris, EISTI, Avenue du Parc, Cergy-Pontoise, France

References

[1] S. P. Lloyd and H. S. Witsenhausen. Weapon allocation is np-complete. In *Proceeding IEEE Summer Simulation Conference*, page 1054 âĂŞ 1058, Reno (USA), 1986.

[2] P. A. Hosein and M. Athans. Preferential defense strategies. part i: The static case. Technical report, MIT Laboratory for Information and Decision Systems with partial support, Cambridge (USA), 1990.

[3] S. Bisht. Hybrid genetic-simulated annealing algorithm for optimal weapon allocation inmultilayer defence scenario. *Defence Sci. J.*, 54(3):395 – 405, 2004.

[4] A. Malhotra and R. K. Jain. Genetic algorithm for optimal weapon allocation in multilayer defence scenario. *Defence Sci. J.*, 51(3):285 – 293, 2001.

[5] O. Karasakal. Air defense missile-target allocation models for a naval task group. *Comput. Oper. Res.*, 35:1759 – 1770, 2008.

[6] F. Johansson and G. Falkman. Sward: System for weapon allocation research & development. *13th Conference on Information Fusion (FUSION)*, 1:1–7, July 2010.

[7] O. Kwon, K. Lee, D. Kang, and S. Park. A branch-and-price algorithm for a targeting problem. *Naval Res. Log.*, 54:732 – 741, 2007.

[8] H. Cai, J. Liu, Y. Chen, and H.Wang. Survey of the research on dynamic weapon-target assignment problem. *J. Syst. Eng. Electron.*, 17(3):559 – 565, 2006.

[9] E. Wacholder. A neural network-based optimization algorithm for the static weapon-target assignment problem. *ORSA J. Comput.*, 1(4):232 – 246, 1989.

[10] K. E. Grant. Optimal resource allocation using genetic algorithms. Technical report, Naval Research Laboratory, Washington (USA), 1993.

[11] H. Lu, H. Zhang, X. Zhang, and R. Han. An improved genetic algorithm for target assignment optimization of naval fleet air defense. In *6th World Cong. Intell. Contr. Autom.*, pages 3401 – 3405, Dalian (China), 2006.

[12] A. C. Cullenbine. A taboo search approach to the weapon assignment model. Master's thesis, Department of Operational Sciences, Air Force Institute of Technology, Hobson Way, WPAFB, OH, 2000.

[13] D. Blodgett, M. Gendreau, F. Guertin, and J. Y. Potvin. A tabu search heuristic for resource management in naval warfare. *J. Heur.*, 9:145 – 169, 2003.

[14] B. Xin, J. Chen, J. Zhang, L. Dou, and Z. Peng. Efficient decision makings for dynamic weapon-target assignment by virtual permutation and tabu search heuristics. *IEEE transaction on systems, man, and cybernetics - Part C: Application and reviews*, 40(6):649 – 662, 2010.

[15] P. A. Hosein and M. Athans. Preferential defense strategies. part ii: The dynamic case. Technical report, MIT Laboratory for Information and Decision Systems with partial support, Cambridge (USA), 1990.

[16] P. A. Hosein, J. T. Walton, and M. Athans. Dynamic weapon-target assignment problems with vulnerable c2 nodes. Technical report, MIT Laboratory for Information and Decision Systems with partial support, Cambridge (USA), 1988.

[17] P. A. Hosein and M. Athans. Some analytical results for the dynamic weapon-target allocation problem. Technical report, MIT Laboratory for Information and Decision Systemswith partial support, 1990.

[18] T. Sikanen. Solving weapon target assignment problem with dynamic programming. Technical report, Mat-2.4108 Independent research projects in applied mathematics, 2008.

[19] L. Wu, C. Xing, F. Lu, and P. Jia. An anytime algorithm applied to dynamic weapon-target allocation problem with decreasing weapons and targets. In *IEEE Congr. Evol. Comput.*, pages 3755 – 3759, Hong Kong (China), 2008.

[20] C. Leboucher, R. Chelouah, P. Siarry, and S. Le Ménec. A swarm intelligence method combined to evolutionary game theory applied to the resources allocation problem. *International Journal of Swarm Intelligence Research*, 3(2):20 – 38, 2012.

[21] H.W. Kuhn. The hungarian method for the assignment problem. *Naval Research Logistics Quarterly*, 2:83 – 97, 1955.

[22] J. Kennedy and R. C. Eberhart. Particle swarm optimization. In *Proceedings of IEEE International Conference on Neural Networks*, pages 1942 – 1948, Piscataway (USA), 1995.

[23] M. Clerc. Discrete particle swarm optimization, illustred by the travelling salesman problem. *New Optimization Techniques in Engineering*, 1:219–239, 2004.

[24] J. Kennedy and R.C. Eberhart. A discrete binary version of the particle swarm algorithm. In *The 1997 IEEE International Conference on Systems, Man, and Cybernetics*, volume 5, pages 4104–4108, Orlando (USA), October 1997.

[25] J. Maynard-Smith. *Evolution and the theory of games*. Cambridge University Press, 1982.

[26] P. Taylor and Jonker L. Evolutionary stable strategies and game dynamics. *Mathematical Bioscience*, 40:145–156, 1978.

[27] C. Leboucher, R. Chelouah, P. Siarry, and S. Le Ménec. A swarm intelligence method combined to evolutionary game theory applied to ressources allocation problem. In *International Conference on Swarm Intelligence*, Cergy (France), June 2011.